I TOOK HER NAME

LESSONS FROM MY JOURNEY INTO VULNERABILITY, AUTHENTICITY, AND FEMINISM

I TOOK HER NAME

SHU MATSUO POST

I TOOK HER NAME

Lessons From My Journey Into Vulnerability, Authenticity, and Feminism

ISBN 978-1-5445-1650-9 *Hardcover*

978-1-5445-1652-3 *Paperback*

978-1-5445-1651-6 *Ebook*

For Tina, who helped me get out of the cage I was trapped in.

Promote gender equality—10 percent of author royalties from this book will be donated to not-for-profits, including WomEnpowered International.

CONTENTS

FOREWORD

"Our identity is partly shaped by recognition or its absence, often by the misrecognition of others."

—CHARLES TAYLOR

As a political scientist, I have spent twenty years researching the impact of various laws in Canada, the UK, the US, Japan, Korea, and Taiwan that limit, in different ways, the choice of last name for individuals who wish to get married. Many still deny the right to individuality, and yet these are pretty advanced democracies. This begs the broader question: if democracy and self-government are premised upon the powerful idea that we are born with free will and the right to self-determination, why do *modern* societies force loving couples into naming choices based on gender inequality?

I had the pleasure of meeting Shu following his presentation for HerStory Japan in February 2020. After one encounter, I knew that I wanted to amplify Shu's voice. We are at a pivotal moment in history when we need courageous men to speak out against social injustice. I was so moved by his journey that I invited him to become an enjoi Diversity & Innovation thought partner and share his experience for a global webinar entitled, "Diversifying the Faces of Inclusive Leadership."

I Took Her Name is a beautifully personal and honest journey about identity and recognition for one's unique individuality, rather than for the sex, gender, race, or other traits confirmed at birth. It reveals the societal pressures that Shu experiences because he was "born a boy" in Japan. Denying his emotions and desire for meaningful connection with women, Shu ultimately experienced an identity crisis. His sense of self no longer felt authentic, and this disconnect opened up to Shu's quest for freedom from the chains of old-fashioned definitions of "manhood."

The personal is political; the political is deeply personal. In attempting to share a last name with his life partner, Shu discovered that this "women's issue," and the goal of feminism is actually to remove the arbitrary limits upon individual freedom, for women and for men. This realization leads him to find the courage of his convictions, and with his partner's support and guidance, he finds his authentic voice, individuality, and name. Shu then invests his free will to fight for *his right* to celebrate the respectful relationship he had carefully created with his wife. That is his right and the right of all men. This display of courage and integrity at such a young age offers great hope for the world.

Through this beautiful book documenting a love of country, a love of freedom, and a love of one's life partner, we get a firsthand account of one man's dedication to making the world a more equal and inclusive place. I am honored to write this foreword in praise of his first book. As a lifelong advocate of equality and diversity, and also as a mother of a girl and boy, I believe that Shu's journey captures the very best of empowered masculinity and inclusive leadership. I hope many men will be inspired by this story, which offers a beacon of hope for the promise of more peaceful gender relations for all of our sons and daughters.

Dr. Jackie F. Steele
International speaker and author
Founder, enjoi Diversity & Innovation

INTRODUCTION

DEAR MEN,

Since childhood, you've been told a lie.

You have been conditioned to believe a story that's full of untruths: a story that manhood is supposed to be a certain way.

In this story, you are the main character. You are described as physically tough. You are stoic and strong. In this story, no crying is allowed. You must be smart, athletic, and financially successful. To achieve your character's goals, you must be dominant, in control, and independent. All. The. Time.

Only because you were born a male.

And let me guess—you, as this character, don't want to follow this narrator's script.

Does this sound familiar?

Because of these expectations, you are lacking deep connection with yourself and others. You may feel like a victim in society.

At times, you feel exhausted, frustrated, resentful, and angry because this is not what you thought your life would be. Perhaps you thought you were playing your role in the "script" perfectly as a man.

You are afraid to start an unscripted life. What if people don't understand you? What if they judge you? What if they turn their backs and abandon you? The act of questioning your role in society might lead to a change you aren't ready to face.

Does this describe you?

If so, then ***this is the perfect book for you.***

I wrote this book specifically for people just like you, as you embark on your journey to confront gender expectations and find freedom in your life.

WHAT YOU WILL GET FROM THIS BOOK

This book will give you a new perspective on masculinity and what it means to be a more vulnerable, emotional, and engaged man. It will help you understand your authentic self, pointing the way toward self-awareness, self-acceptance, and love of yourself.

I hope that, as you read these pages, you will first acknowledge how gender expectations in your culture form major roadblocks, preventing you from becoming the person you truly want to be. Then, you will understand that showing vulnerability is a sign of strength, a revelation that will lead you toward a life that's most authentic to you.

Through shifting your mindset in this fashion, you will start to remove the frustration, shame, and anger from your life. This will allow you to discover your true self and develop meaningful relationships with others by releasing yourself from the pressure and expectations of being "the man" in your culture.

WHO AM I TO TELL YOU ALL OF THIS?

This is the part where I'm supposed to explain why I am the expert and authority on this subject. Unlike most successful authors in this field, I don't have a PhD in masculinity. Nor do I have a connection with Brené Brown I could leverage to research men and shame, or a podcast about achieving greatness with millions of listeners, like Lewis Howes.

In fact, I don't even have a college degree in gender studies.

But I do have a unique story.

I took my wife's last name.

A 2018 study of recently married American men showed that a mere 3 percent took their wife's last name.[1] The same study found that, of those with an advanced degree, not a single one of the men surveyed changed their name. Why? Those men found themselves in the traditional breadwinner role. Potentially, they had more to *lose* by changing their surname.

My name is Shu Matsuo Post. And I'm probably the first man with an MBA to tell you how much I've *gained* from changing my surname after my marriage. Through my name-changing journey, I've gotten a glimpse into a woman's world. This new perspective has given me the courage to confront gender expectations, embrace vulnerability, and find a level of freedom I didn't even know I could achieve.

---

1 "Marriage name game: What kind of guy would take his wife's last name?" Portland State University, published May 10, 2018, https://phys.org/news/2018-05-marriage-game-kind-guy-wife.html.

No, you don't need to change your last name to achieve this. But you do need to be comfortable talking about the new F-Word: Feminism.

If I asked you whether you believe in gender equality, what would you say? I can picture most of you nodding. If you answered yes, here is another question. Are you a feminist?

Now, most of you are probably shaking your head.

You are not alone. You are actually the majority. According to a 2018 study, only 10 percent of American male millennials identified themselves as feminists. Although I'm not American, I did not identify myself as a feminist until a few years ago.

Now, I do. Yes, that's right. I *am* a feminist.

I always thought that I believed in gender equality but viewed the idea of feminism negatively. I thought it was a word used to describe angry, hairy, man-hating women, or submissive, nonmasculine men. I didn't make the association between gender equality and feminism.

First, let me introduce myself. I am a tall, athletic Japanese man with a husky voice. I lift weights and play sports with my friends. I'm attracted to feminine women.

I am a manly man. I belong to the man's club.

Well, that's how I used to position myself as a man.

Due to the limited view I grew up with, I didn't even give feminism a chance. But as I became more aware of the subject and went through my name-changing process, my perspective started to change drastically.

WHY DID I WRITE THIS BOOK?

Graduating from university with a journalism degree, I've always enjoyed writing, and publishing a book was part of my life's vision since I was little. I see writing as a way to leave a legacy when I'm gone from this world. I want my children, grandchildren, and great-grandchildren to know what type of person I was when they grow up. My maternal grandparents passed away within the first year I was born. My mom keeps telling me that they were happy to meet me before they passed, but I have no memory of them. When I got older, my parents told me more about who they were so I started to understand them, but it's hard to relate, since I didn't get to know them directly. I wish my ancestors wrote books so I could connect with them even if they are not alive.

More importantly, I wanted to write because I knew I wanted to communicate with people outside of my family and get the message out to the world. I believe that my story can help you find your *why*. It took me a few years to find the freedom I was looking for. I hope you find yours in a few hours.

While I always wanted to publish a book, I never thought I would write one about my journey with changing my birth name. Steve Jobs said, "If you are working on something you really care about, you don't have to be pushed. The vision pulls you." I started writing because I became so passionate about finding my voice and sharing my story. As I reflected on my experience, I felt a burning curiosity about *why* gender roles are often so fixed. So, I read books and articles related to the subject of gender equality. No one pushed me to do this. My vision pulled me to make my story into this book. I wrote this book because I want to share my experience of gender inequality in the country I grew up in and love so deeply, and how I escaped from the cage in which I was trapped.

So why the heck am I writing about Japan in English? I just happen to have grown up in Japan. What I've experienced could have happened anywhere in the world. You don't need to have any connection with Japan because gender inequality is a global issue. So, if you've made it this far, keep reading. If you make it to the end, do me a favor and pass this book on to your male friends or partner(s). I'm writing this to all English-speaking men who are open to finding the truth in their own stories.

This book is about why every man should confront gender expectations and embrace vulnerability to live his life fully.

Truthfully, I hope my future grandchildren will pick up this book and laugh at the bunch of nonsense remarks I've made here. "People used to assume things about others because of what genitals they were born with? That's stupid," the future generation will say. Quite frankly, that's my goal. I want the future to be more equal than today.

If you're not a feminist already, this book will not make you one. That's completely up to you to decide. ***But when you do commit to becoming one, you will experience a freedom you have never known before.***

What does feminism have to do with men achieving freedom? It has to do with uncovering the truth about manhood. You will only be able to experience this truth if you decide to test the waters, defy the worries of others, and discover your true story.

Now, it's time to uncover the truth about feminism, through sharing my story. I hope you, too, will uncover truths about your relationship with masculinity as you join me on this journey. Are you ready?

WHAT YOU'LL FIND IN THESE PAGES

This book is divided into four parts. The first part is a collection of stories that have led me to believe that feminism means fighting for gender equality. Growing up in Japan, then living in the US and Hong Kong for most of my adolescence and young adult life, I suffered an identity crisis. I didn't feel that I belonged to any particular culture or group, so I didn't know who I was supposed to be. In the US and Hong Kong, I was a minority by nationality.

In my mind, equality was the foundation of connection and belonging. But when it came to equality between women and men, I knew very little. I never had the opportunity to see the world through a woman's perspective. Or maybe I did, but I subconsciously chose not to acknowledge this issue.

I didn't know what feminism was, nor how gender unequal the world is because I had a fixed story in my head about what manhood was supposed to mean.

Part I of this book is about my own journey toward feminism through the personal experience of taking my wife's name. This part of the book details my stories and is divided into three chapters:

- Chapter 1 is about how I viewed the world before I took my wife's name.

- Chapter 2 is about what I experienced during my name-changing process.
- Chapter 3 is about how the name-changing process helped me see this world from a woman's perspective, which eventually transformed me into a feminist.

After Part I, the focus shifts to gender issues around the world. You may not have any connection with Japan, so you may wonder whether my experience in my home country accurately reflects gender inequality around the world.

In Part II of the book, I'll demonstrate that gender inequality exists everywhere, even in the most liberal countries on the planet. I'll show you how, as we lift this veil, we open a portal to a deeper, richer life. Part II details stories of women. It is divided into two chapters:

- Chapter 4 is about systemic sexism and how we live in a world that favors men.
- Chapter 5 is about how gender inequality affects women in the workplace.

Before this transformative journey began, I was subconsciously living my life with the intention of meeting societal expectations. Although I didn't like it, I didn't have the courage to live an unscripted life. I didn't know how to confront the assumptions and patterns I saw all around me. But when I discovered why those gender expectations existed, I found a solution.

Part III details stories of men. It is divided into two chapters:

- Chapter 6 is about how we got to where we are today.
- Chapter 7 is about how we view masculinity and how it affects us.

Albert Einstein said, "If I had an hour to solve a problem, I'd spend fifty-five minutes thinking about the problem and five minutes thinking about solutions." The third part of this book is about the problems.

Finally, Part IV of this book is about finding solutions to gender inequality. In this part, you will learn how to confront gender expectations, finding the freedom to let go and live the life you truly desire.

Like any other transformation, however, this one will require you to take action. I know I'm not the first man to passionately talk about gender equality. There are many men who care deeply about this topic. But caring deeply is not enough. It must be followed by a commitment to consistent action.

This part of the book also consists of two chapters:

- Chapter 8 is about confronting the expectations society places upon us.
- Chapter 9 is about shifting our mindset to believe we can break free of those expectations.

Are you scared to mess it all up? It's OK. We are all going to make mistakes. But we can't stay silent. Martin Luther King Jr. said, "In the end, we will remember not the words of our enemies but the silence of our friends."

Men, I know you care about the women and girls in your lives who didn't choose to live in a society that values men above women only because we were born a certain way. I know you also care about our young men and boys who don't know how to become the men they want to be in a culture that tells them manhood means following rigid codes of behavior.

Fortunately, we do have a choice. We can take responsibility for working with women to rewrite the script for future generations.

Part IV is a call to arms. No more silence. It's time to speak up and share our stories together.

Now, let's get this journey started. We've got a train to catch.

PART I

MY STORY

WHY I TOOK HER NAME

CHAPTER 1

BEFORE I TOOK HER NAME

"The truth will set you free, but first it will piss you off."

—GLORIA STEINEM

SUMMER 2009, TOKYO, JAPAN

I want to tell you a story about a twenty-three-year-old nonconformist who avoided conflict with others at all costs. He was probably the last person on earth you would ever look to for advice on how to break societal rules.

Which is why he is the perfect place to start.

This young man was living and working in Tokyo in 2009. One humid summer day, he worked a late shift. When the shift ended, he decided to go for drinks with his coworkers.

In Japan, many workers go out for dinner and drinks after work, even on weekdays. "Work hard, play hard," they say.

When the man realized it was 11 p.m., he quickly excused himself from the group to make his way back home. He got off a subway train to catch a transitioning one. He only had a few stops to go, but the train he wanted to catch was still ten minutes away. More people smelling like alcohol were walking up to the platform. Although it was late, many people were trying to rush home before the last train, which left around midnight.

When the train arrived at the station, the car the young man wanted to board was jam-packed. Even though he was used to being packed like a sardine in a can on his journey to work every day, he preferred to avoid that indignity on his journey home.

You may have seen footage of insanely packed Japanese trains during rush hours. It's an everyday occurrence in Tokyo. Station workers wearing white gloves stand ready to shove people in so that doors can close. In a country where people don't even have enough sex to sustain the population, they crowd into impossibly cramped quarters with strangers every day on the train.

This story takes place in a time before cordless headsets. People still reached into their pockets to skip songs on their iPods. In a packed train at rush hour, this was nearly impossible. Those who had enough space to reach into their pockets during rush hour felt it was their lucky day.

Eager to escape the crush, the young man quickly moved to the next car and jumped on as the train doors closed. *This car isn't even full,* he thought to himself. *I could listen to my iPod and skip songs.* As he swerved between other passengers, he put his hands in his pockets.

That's when a strange incident occurred.

The man leaned against a door, looking at his iPod screen as he chose a playlist. He was tired from working all day, and the couple of drinks at dinner were making him sleepy. As he closed his eyes and let himself enjoy the soothing music, he felt a vigorous tap on his shoulder.

"Hey, you!" a middle-aged woman yelled at him. "What are you doing here? Get out of here!"

Shocked, he looked up and realized that the woman's eyebrows were shaped like an angry cartoon character. Confused, he looked around the train car. He saw other passengers staring at him like he was a criminal. They were all women—he was the only man in the car. From the looks on their faces, he imagined they were silently accusing him of being a pervert.

He had blundered into a women-only car.

"*Sumimasen!*" Embarrassed, the young man apologized loudly enough for the passengers around him to hear and ran to the next car. This second car was full of men, who looked up from their *Manga* magazines long enough to shoot him a glance that meant "poor idiot."

The young man was deeply ashamed. Accidentally, he had broken a deeply embedded rule. The thought that others might mistake him for someone who would make others sexually uncomfortable was horrifying. Admittedly, he was a little bit tipsy from the alcohol, but he still had enough of his wits about him to know he hadn't wandered into an imaginary matriarchal world where women had more social power than men and wrote the rules.

It was real life.

In his packed car, people looked at the man sympathetically but didn't say anything. He hoped they were thinking, *This guy doesn't seem like a groper. He's just an idiot who accidentally walked into a women-only car.*

The sad, underlying truth of this story is that women-only train cars serve an important function in Japan. Men groping women on packed train cars is still a major social issue in this country.

Many men appreciate these barriers because they don't need to worry about false accusations of groping. The 2007 film *I Just Didn't Do It*, which portrays a young man who was falsely accused of groping a woman on a train, became a national sensation.

It was even nominated for the Best Foreign Language Film at the Academy Awards the same year. When this movie came out, many parents, including my mom, worried about their sons taking packed trains. It was ironic, given that women had been dealing with the fear of being groped for decades.

The initiative to provide women-only train cars in Japan started in 2001. Today, many Japanese train companies enforce women-only passenger cars during rush hours or even throughout the day. While many other countries have withdrawn gender-specific public services, Japan continues to provide women-only cars.

Oh, and the guy I mentioned earlier?

That was me.

Welcome to the world of gender inequality. The following are stories from my childhood to early adulthood that shaped my view on feminism before I took my wife's name.

CHILDHOOD

MANY YEARS AGO, KANAGAWA, JAPAN

According to my parents, I was born as Shohei Matsuo. They named me Shohei, but my grandmother thought Shuhei sounded better, so that became my official first name. If my mom had kept her maiden name and my dad had taken her last name when they got married, my last name would have been Ogawa, but she followed the social norm in Japan and took his surname.

My older brother and I were raised by loving parents in an ordinary home in a suburb of Tokyo. When my brother was born, my parents were both working, but after I arrived, my mom decided to take care of us full time. My dad became the main breadwinner of our household and often arrived home only after the three of us had finished dinner. He commuted over an hour each way to and from Tokyo to be the sole provider for the family.

While I understand that my parents made a choice for my mom to take the primary caregiver's role and for my dad to take the primary provider's role, it seemed natural to me. Based on my observations of my friends' families, I thought that was what married women and men usually did.

I admire my parents for taking the best possible care of my brother and me. My mom ran the show around the house, taking care of her two boys and my dad with healthy, organic meals. We rarely ate out, not because we couldn't afford it, but because my mom believed that a healthy life starts with healthy eating.

My dad was a hardworking business owner who doubled as my baseball and golf coach. He has been in the golf industry for most of his career. When I was old enough to pick up a sport, he taught me how to swing a club. When weekends rolled around, I looked forward to visiting his golf shop in the neighboring town and practicing at the driving range next door. He was also a writer and often wrote articles for golf magazines in Japan. He maintained an office inside his golf shop so he could write when he wasn't selling golf clubs to his customers.

One day, my dad got a big opportunity. He was offered the chance to write a report on an up-and-coming golf company based in San Diego, California. He decided to combine this business trip to the US with a vacation for our family. That vacation was my first international trip, which ended up leading to annual trips to San Diego for several years to come. These vacations permanently changed the way I saw the world.

SUMMER 1991, CARLSBAD, CALIFORNIA, USA

"This is the biggest omelet I've ever seen in my life!"

When I first experienced the taste of America at the Olympic Resort Hotel & Spa, I was six years old. It was also my very first trip outside of Japan. My dad worked for a company that was and still is based in Carlsbad, so he used to take my mom, my brother, and me to Southern California nearly every summer from 1991 to 2000.

Everything was so different in the US—the smell of the air, the spaciousness, the massive portions of food at restaurants. You name it. I was completely fascinated with American culture.

"I'm going to move here one day."

I made that decision at the age of six, and every trip we made to San Diego amplified my desire to make my dream come true. All I could think of was the way everything in America was BIG. Want to become the best athlete in the world? Go to America. Want to be the wealthiest person in the world? Go to America. Want to fulfill your greatest potential? Go to America. My six-year-old self firmly believed that the United States was the greatest country in the world, and I needed to be there.

In 2001, my dream became a reality. Yet, I had no idea about the cultural differences I would experience as a foreigner.

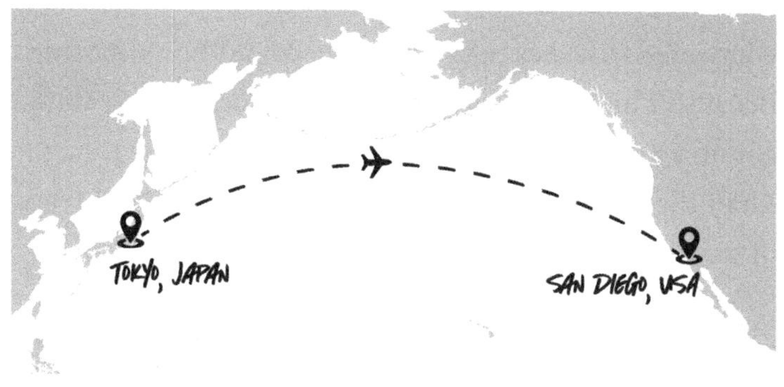

ADOLESCENCE

2001–2009, USA

I grew up in a homogenous country. By that, I mean every single person looked the same, believed the same, and behaved the same. That's not necessarily a bad thing, but it didn't serve me well when I moved to San Diego at the age of fifteen and spent the next eight and a half years in the US.

When I was growing up, I never had any friends who were different from me. All my friends were basically carbon copies of me, which made anything else unique. Even though all the differences were new to me, which at times was scary, meeting people from all around the world, with different skin colors, religions, and sexual orientations was exciting.

Living in San Diego, Los Angeles, and New York opened my eyes. As a Japanese foreigner in the US, I felt especially connected to issues relating to race and other minorities. Because I had experienced being a majority in my home country and a minority in a different country, I thought I had the empathy to connect with people from all types of backgrounds.

My assumption could not have been further from the truth. When I decided to go home, I couldn't even fully reconnect to the culture in which I grew up.

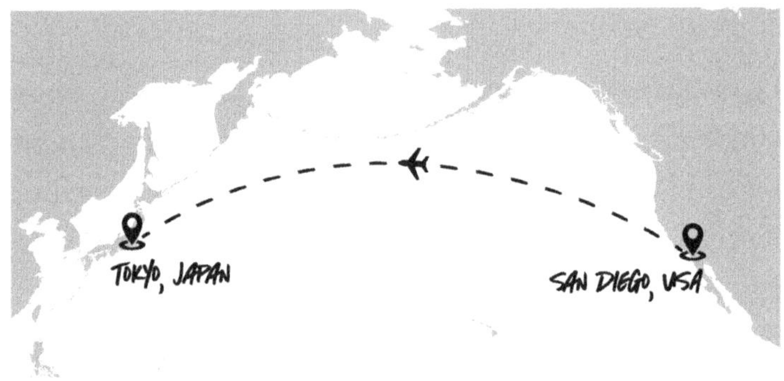

EARLY ADULTHOOD

2009–2012, JAPAN

After spending nearly a decade of my adolescence in the US, I moved back to Japan as a young professional. At first, I was excited to rediscover the culture in which I grew up, but I experienced a high level of reverse culture shock. As I readjusted to the culture and values of my home country, I dealt with unexpected difficulties. The previously familiar had become unfamiliar.

By the time I returned to Japan, I had spent more than one-third of my life in the US. On the inside, I was no longer a "typical" Japanese person. While my appearance and my ability to speak Japanese had remained almost the same since I left home eight years prior, my internal values were mixed up like a California roll. After spending a crucial developmental period in international cities full of diversity, I was forced to reassess the homogenous culture in which I grew up. After living eight years of my life as a racial minority and a foreigner, I had a completely different perspective on life.

I looked the same as other people in Japan, but I didn't *feel* the same. That was when the truth hit me; I had become a minority in my own country. How was this even possible? In case you're not familiar with Japanese culture, let me explain.

Social expectations in Japan are quite rigid. For example, it's considered bad manners to talk on the phone on the train. Bowing to others is a way to show respect. People who look and behave like non-Japanese, however, are not expected to conform as tightly to these expectations. We Japanese have a highly sensitive radar for differentiating between Japanese and non-Japanese, including other Asians. We are like a QR code reader app—most people think every QR code looks the same, but a QR code reader knows every one of them is different.

Taking advantage of the fact that one is not Japanese is called pulling a *gaijin* (foreigner) card. The difficulty of pulling a *gaijin* card depends heavily on how Japanese a person looks. A person like Emma Stone, no matter how "Japanese" she behaves, looks fundamentally different from a typical Japanese person. Therefore, she can automatically pull a *gaijin* card. If someone looks like Lucy Liu, on the other hand, but behaves like she grew up in Japan, she will have a tougher time pulling a *gaijin* card. The more non-Japanese people appear, the more easily they can use this method.

For someone like me, this presents a considerable challenge. I am Japanese, look Japanese, and therefore presumably know how to behave Japanese. Yet, following my return from the US, my values weren't completely Japanese. A part of me was more American. You might expect the clothing brand Superdry to be somewhat Japanese because the logo contains some Japanese characters, but it's actually a British brand. How you look doesn't represent who you are as a whole person. It's just one element of what makes you a person.

In one of the most homogenous countries in the world, I struggled to fit into a culture that values conformity over individuality. In Japan, we have a saying, *deru kugi wa utareru*, which means "a nail that sticks out gets hammered down." On my return to Japan, I felt like I was a tall nail that was sticking out, and society was trying to hammer me down.

As an example, let me tell you about an unforgettable moment that took place while I was a manager at a flagship store of an American retail brand in Tokyo. My team was predominantly female, and there were many female managers above me. However, none of them spoke Japanese. When we received complaint calls from local customers and the problem was deemed "too important" for the phone operator to solve, customers asked to speak to a male superior. That person was usually me.

One specific customer asked for "a male manager who is Japanese." I responded by saying, "That would be me. I was born and raised in Japan. How can I help?" Even though I spoke Japanese and we could communicate with each other, this customer questioned my authenticity because he thought my Japanese sounded foreign.

This customer expected the authority figure of an American company in Japan to be a Japanese man who was fluent in *keigo*, the honorific form of Japanese, which the natives start learning in junior high school. I identified myself as Japanese, so I was automatically disqualified from pulling a *gaijin* card. Therefore, the customer expected me to be fluent in *keigo*.

I was deeply frustrated. First, this customer flat-out disrespected women by requesting to speak to a male authority figure, implying that women weren't good enough for him to speak to. Second, he gave me the impression I didn't belong in my home country because I didn't follow the cultural script I was given at birth.

This one example illustrates a much larger problem I encountered in Japan. Outwardly, I was home, but I desperately wanted to be a foreigner in my own country. I was frustrated by the cultural norms I felt obliged to observe. I held a Japanese passport and wasn't yet married to a foreign partner, so it seemed as though I had few outlets for escaping my frustration. I kept wondering if there was anyone like me with whom I could share my pain. There was only one solution: working on my *gaijin* card skills.

During this time, there was one guy I looked up to, although his background wasn't quite like mine. He was a Japanese American with a Japanese name. He spoke more eloquent English than me, yet his Japanese was a little more broken. He was a master of pulling a *gaijin* card and used it effectively to advance in his career in Japan.

For example, if he was on a phone call, he would say in Japanese, "I'm sorry, I am Japanese, but I grew up in America. I speak Japanese well enough, but I don't want to offend you with my limited *keigo*. Do you mind me helping you in English?" If the customer said yes, my friend would continue in English and would demonstrate a high level of problem-solving skills in his native language. Even if the customer said no, he would be impressed with my friend's Japanese because he would now know that he wasn't a native Japanese speaker.

My friend was fully aware of his limitations. He understood that there was a clear difference between how society would treat him as a Japanese native and a Japanese American. He knew that he could leverage his Americanness to manage expectations. This is the art of pulling a *gaijin* card as a Japanese individual.

I, on the other hand, struggled with this art. Even though I was born and raised in Japan, I had spent nearly a decade—most of my adolescence—in the US. I felt like I was partly American, and I looked and behaved that way. Yet, I felt guilty fully expressing my identity at the time. "I don't have an American passport and I'm not even native in English," I would tell myself. "Who am I?" I felt as though I had lost my identity, like kids who went to many different international schools because their parents frequently moved to other countries for work.

Japan is a homogenous culture where cultural expectations are often black and white. People are either Japanese or not Japanese. A woman or a man. Fluent in English or not at all. The interesting part is that Japanese society pressures everyone to learn English. It's a mandatory subject in the public education system, starting in middle school. Yet, even with six to ten years of formal English education, it is very rare for someone who grew up with public education in Japan to be able to speak conversational English. This is because Japan treats English more like a subject rather than a language. For many locals, it's an impractical language they study in school. In a Japanese person, fluency in English is an indication that they have lived abroad at some point in their life. To others in their society, they appear to be foreigners or *kikokushijo*, repatriate children.

When I first moved back to Japan in 2009, many people mistook me for a *kikokushijo*, even though I did not move to the US due to my parents' work. When I explained that I studied abroad in America by choice, people often became confused. In their minds, studying abroad was usually a one-year exchange program.

So, when people found out that I *just* studied abroad, their reaction was, "What has America done to you?" as though some of my Japanese-ness was sucked out of me by the time I spent in the US. For the two and a half years I was back in Japan from 2009 to 2012, life in my own country was not easy for me. I felt that I had lost my identity in the culture where I grew up.

Looking back, it's clear that this thought process was a story inside my head. I created my reality from my uncomfortable collision with Japanese culture after living abroad for eight years. At the time, I did not fully take responsibility for my reactions in this situation. I thought that if I left Japan again, the problem would be solved. The story in my head led me to my desire to leave the country.

And so, it happened. After two and a half years in Tokyo, I took an opportunity to move to Hong Kong.

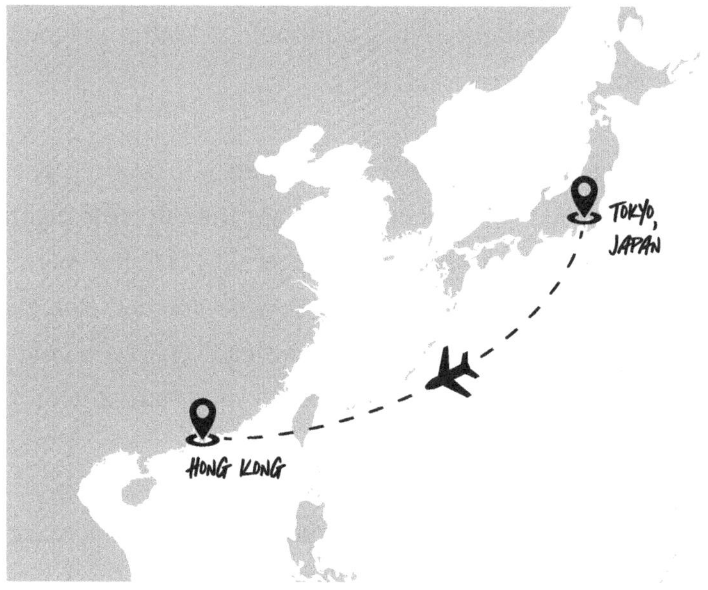

ADULTHOOD

2012–2017, HONG KONG, CHINA

Moving to Hong Kong was the single most pivotal decision

of my whole life for one reason: toward the end of my five-year stay, I finally found my identity.

When I accepted an offer from my employer to relocate to Hong Kong, I did not know much about the city; only that it was part of China and that my parents spent their twenty-fifth wedding anniversary there when I was a teenager. From the day I signed my contract until the day I moved to a completely new city, I had two weeks, so I got online and learned everything I could about Hong Kong. Usually, this part comes *before* signing any contract, but I was so excited about living abroad again that I signed first and did my research later.

My life in Hong Kong was vibrant and exhilarating. The city is only four hours from Tokyo, yet the culture is night and day. It's like New York City on steroids. I felt the energy and motivation coming out of everyone walking through the city. Hong Kong is a city that never sleeps, even more so than Tokyo. For those who like to work hard and play harder, it's a mecca.

For me, the most exciting part about being in Hong Kong was that I got to be a foreigner again. Initially, I was nervous about learning a new language. Cantonese is one of the hardest languages to speak, with nine different tones. In Hong Kong, however, everyone speaks English, so I got away without learning Cantonese. Although I learned a few phrases on my first day, people didn't even bother to respond to me in Cantonese.

This is amazing, I thought. At the same time, I wondered why everyone in Hong Kong spoke English so well. Was it the education or the East-meets-West environment? I thought that if Japan could learn how to teach English from Hong Kong, life would be so much easier for many people.

Hong Kong changed my life in the way a radioactive spider bite changed Peter Parker's life in *Spider-Man*. I got bitten by this bug and became addicted to the city's energy. As a self-proclaimed ambivert, I had never been particularly outgoing. During my first two years in Hong Kong, however, I socialized probably more than during my previous twenty-five years combined. I drank more alcohol in those two years than I had in my entire life. I ate more mints at work than hours I worked on the retail floor. I went out partying on more weeknights than rest days. I blacked out and threw up more than I'd like to admit. I thought sleeping was for losers. I even got a tattoo that says, "Sleep when I'm dead." Ironically, sleeping is now one of my favorite activities.

I thought I was celebrating my freedom from oppressive cultural expectations. No one had cultural expectations of me because I came from Japan, and being a foreigner was such a norm in this city. I met and became friends with a diverse group of people from all parts of Asia, Europe, Africa, Oceania, and North America, as well as people of different sexual orientations.

Living such a sociable life in the heart of Hong Kong, arguably the most diverse place in Asia, I thought I was open-minded. It was a similar feeling I had when I first came back to Japan after living in the US for eight years; I had felt open-minded in comparison to other Japanese people. With my rich experience of diversity, I thought I could connect with any group of people. With one exception: women.

No matter where I lived in the world, I didn't seem to connect deeply with the women in my life. I had relationships with women, but none of them lasted more than a year. All the romantic relationships I had in my first two years in Hong Kong felt transactional. There was a reason why I couldn't sustain a romantic relationship longer than a year: I had never attempted to see the world from a woman's perspective.

In hindsight, I was holding subconscious gender bias. I thought I needed to behave a certain way to attract women. I created stories in my head about how a successful, heterosexual romantic relationship should be. Evidently, my threshold for playing the role I mapped out for myself was about a year. After that, my authentic self couldn't keep up with the lies I was telling myself.

Luckily, my life started to change when I met my future wife, who helped me see the world from a female perspective and eventually taught me the meaning of equality of the sexes. My journey to feminism, however, didn't start on the day we met. It was a gradual process that began on September 11, 2014.

FALL 2014, HONG KONG, CHINA

"So, what was your birthday like in 2001?" I asked as if no one had ever asked her the question before.

Ever since I found out that my girlfriend's birthday was on 9/11, I had been meaning to ask the question. I'm not usually good with people's birthdays, but this one was hard to forget.

"I remember walking down the hall with my friends towards second-period social studies class and seeing the TVs on in every classroom," she recalled. "The tragedy of the day was intense, but secretly, my fifteen-year-old self was sad that no one remembered my birthday."

On this particular evening, her twenty-eighth birthday, I took her out for what would be the first of many birthday celebrations together. At that time, we had only been dating for a few months. Wanting to demonstrate my chivalry, I made reservations at a steakhouse on Wyndham Street in the heart of downtown Hong Kong and made plans for us to drink cocktails on the rooftop of Sevva, overlooking the bright lights of the city. I was pumped. I wore my trendy skinny tie and my buttoned-down shirt that subtly accented my pecs. In my mind, she was going to proclaim me, "Boyfriend of the Year."

We walked into the steakhouse, and I immediately pulled out her chair so she could take a seat at the white-clothed table. She looked around, feeling slightly out of place, but I beamed at the luxury of it all. As the waiter approached, I ordered a bottle of fine red wine, her favorite, and went about recommending the most expensive items on the menu. We normally ate at local noodle shops and small restaurants aimed at expats in Central and we always split the bill, so I was on cloud nine. I was treating my lady right on her special day.

As the evening progressed, however, the conversation took an unexpected turn. The food was great, and the wine was excellent, but my girlfriend wasn't all that impressed with the chivalry. On top of that, she had just started teaching her annual Language and Gender unit to her twelfth graders at school, and she started asking me more about my thoughts on the topic. Where did my sense of male obligation come from? Why do men feel the need to pay for women all the time? Why did I order for her when the waiter came over rather than let her order for herself? My mind reeled. Her tone was gentle, but her words stung. I honestly didn't know the answer to her questions.

We continued to debate the topic, and she schooled me thoroughly. She clearly knew what she was talking about, whereas I was scrambling to defend the male sex. At one point, I argued that men experience gender bias too and that men are just as likely to be discriminated against as women. I was convinced that the idea of women getting paid less than men was false, and I was sure that the patriarchy was a lie. This did not go over well. I couldn't see her side of the argument and later found myself looking on Wikipedia, desperate to find the source of my "male discrimination" argument just to make my point. Meanwhile, back at her apartment, she sat with her arms folded, waiting for me to find what I was looking for. I never found it, but I wasn't ready to concede.

Shortly afterward, Emma Watson gave her famous HeForShe speech at the UN. I had been ruminating over the conversation I had with my girlfriend on her birthday and found myself watching the speech countless times. It was undeniable that my girlfriend's arguments were based on more than just her opinion.

This speech was the catalyst for me to begin understanding feminism. I realized that a feminist is *"a person who believes in the social, political, and economic equality of the sexes."* A feminist doesn't mean someone who hates men, as I had initially thought. One can wear a short dress and high heels and love men and still be a feminist. A feminist acknowledges that there are unequal gaps between genders and works toward closing them.

I began to open up to my girlfriend about my lack of understanding, and she approached these conversations with sensitivity, openness, and a willingness to help me find meaning. I started to notice many gender-unequal situations in my life. For example, why is it usually women who change their last name after getting married? A study shows that around 94 percent of women in the US take their husband's last name after marriage.[2] If society was already equal, why wouldn't that number be near 50 percent?

The more I thought about inequality in society, the more issues I noticed around the world.

Why do men get paid more than their female counterparts for doing the same work?

---

2 Emily Fitzgibbons Shafer, "Hillary Rodham Versus Hillary Clinton: Consequences of Surname Choice in Marriage," published January 4, 2017, https://link.springer.com/article/10.1007/s12147-016-9182-5?shared-article-renderer.

Why do most languages have more words to insult women?

Why are there overwhelmingly more stay-at-home moms than dads?

What would be the benefits of achieving gender equality for men?

Two years later, after following my masculine script, getting down on one knee and popping the question on a beach in New Zealand, I decided I needed to walk the walk. I needed to start actively changing my story. I decided that when my girlfriend became my wife, I would change my name. This may sound simple in today's Western society, but keep in mind, I'm a Japanese native, and Japanese people are not known for throwing out the gender script. In the Global Gender Gap Index 2020 rankings, Japan is ranked #121 of 153 countries, and it breaks my heart to know that such a beautiful country is so many years behind the rest of the world.

In the summer of 2017, my wife and I got married in the US and moved to Japan, ending our five-year stay in Hong Kong.

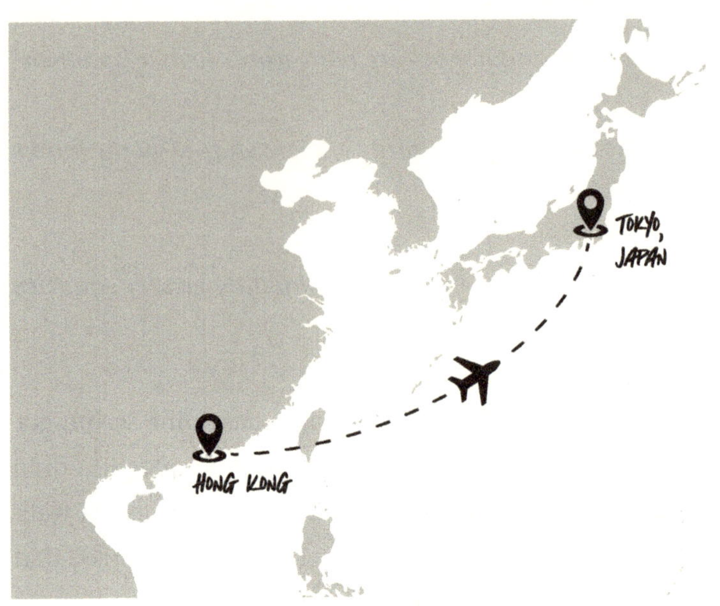
TOKYO,
JAPAN
HONG KONG

CHAPTER 2

WHEN I TOOK HER NAME

"Privilege is invisible to those who have it."

—MICHAEL KIMMEL

What does taking my wife's last name have to do with male privilege?

We'll get there. First, let's start with a short history of last names.

Until quite recently, humans didn't use surnames. The adoption of surnames happened at different times in different cultures. In China, family names go back so far that they are explained by a legend. One early use of surnames came almost 5,000 years ago from a Chinese emperor named Fu Xi, who implemented the family name system.

Originally, people took their mothers' names. Around the twelfth century BCE, however, they started using their fathers' names. These names came from many places, including a dynasty's name, a person's title, and a person's occupation. Reputedly, this is why the majority of Chinese still share a small number of surnames today, despite the country's massive population of 1.4 billion people.

In Japan and Korea, there were no last names until around 1900. In Korea, most last names were borrowed from the Chinese. In Japan, people chose their names or asked their priests to give them their names.

In ancient Greece, people were only known by their first names before 500 BCE. Last names were introduced to identify people in Athens. The politician Cleisthenes set up a system in which people were officially known by their region in addition to their name. Last names evolved from this system.

In the Roman Empire, people were originally known by a single name. Eventually, Romans ended up having three names: praenomen, nomen, and cognomen. A praenomen was a name parents gave children; a nomen identified the person's clan; and a cognomen was either a nickname or a hereditary name.

In the English-speaking part of the world, it wasn't until

around 1066, after the Normans conquered the Britons, that last names became common. The English developed four ways to define a surname—by occupation, hometown, nickname, or baptismal name. Occupations gave us names like Baker, Taylor, and Smith. Names derived from locations include Moore, Hill, and Wood. Blunt and Fox are examples of nicknames. Finally, baptismal names descend from the father, so someone whose father is named William may call himself Williams or Williamson.[3]

Now, a little history about my birth name.

My birth name Matsuo literally means pine tree (Matsu) tail (o). It is believed that it came from Kyushu as most Matsuos live on the westmost major island of Japan. Growing up, my surname wasn't overly unique or popular. That changed when the baseball star Hideki Matsui moved to the US to play for the New York Yankees in 2003. I was already in the US at the time and ever since he became a sensation in the MLB, some people started to call me Matsui. It got worse when Kazuo Matsui also began to play in the MLB the following year. Unlike Suzuki, Matsui is not a very common name in Japan, but when two Japanese baseball players with the name broke out in the US in consecutive years, people assumed that it must be. Hence,

---

3 Mental Floss, "Where Did Last Names Come From?" *Big Questions* (Ep. 8), YouTube, uploaded October 20, 2014, https://www.youtube.com/watch?v=Q3AJZfrlWUQ.

more people called me Matsui than Matsuo until I moved back to Japan in 2009.

On the other hand, my wife's maiden name is Post, which came from her father, who is originally from Switzerland. My wife wanted to keep her last name because it had been her identity for nearly three decades of her life. It told her story. It represented her family.

During our engagement, she told me that she wasn't going to take my last name when we got married because giving up her last name meant a loss of her identity. I didn't expect her to drop her surname and become Matsuo, because I knew how important her name was to her. I, too, felt that it was important to keep my surname because it expressed my identity. We also wanted our future children to have the same last name as us. So, we talked about what to do. The answer was easy; we decided to combine our names so that our children can also have the same last name as us. We decided not to hyphenate the two names because we wanted the option to omit either of them, depending on the situation, and so that our children can choose to do whatever they want when or if they decide to get married and change their names.

For example, in her teaching life, my wife still goes by Ms. Post because it's easier for her students to pronounce, and it was her professional identity prior to our marriage.

In the US, changing our names was a simple process. My wife and I got married in California, and all we needed to do to combine our names was to tell city hall we wanted to do it and sign our marriage certificate. So that's what we did.

In Japan, the process was a lot more challenging. As I write, Japan still doesn't allow a married couple to have different surnames.[4] When people get married in Japan, one of them needs to change their surname to match their spouses'. This situation is discouraging many people in Japan, especially women, from getting married. In Japan, combining our two last names seemed an impossible feat, but that didn't stop us from trying to achieve it.

In the spring of 2018, I officially changed my surname to Matsuo Post. That's my name on my Japanese passport, driver's license, health insurance card, credit cards, airline mileage cards, and every other form of identification. I changed my Facebook and LinkedIn profiles and work and personal email addresses. Changing my name was extremely challenging and required numerous visits to the ward office and the family court in Japan.

Who would have thought? Not me. Of course, I wouldn't

4 The Mainichi, "Tokyo court rejects compensation claim over ban on different surnames for spouses," published March 25, 2019, https://mainichi.jp/english/articles/20190325/p2a/00m/0na/006000c.

have thought about it because I'm a man, and changing names is predominantly done by women.

Due to the patriarchal nature of Japan, the system is not set up for men to easily alter their last names. The intense legal and systematic processes opened my eyes to how often we expect women to make sacrifices in the name of patriarchy. It made me aware of my male privilege. Here is the process I undertook.

HOW I TOOK HER NAME

SUMMER 2017, KANAGAWA, JAPAN

It was the first Friday since my wife and I returned to Japan. We had just moved back to Japan from Hong Kong, our home for the previous five years. To get married in my home country, I needed to go to my hometown's city hall for registration, where I kept my *koseki* or family registry. My wife and I spent a few hours looking for apartments in Yokohama, then took the train back to my hometown. It had been over a year and a half since our previous visit.

My dad picked us up at the station and drove to the ward office of my hometown. We arrived shortly before it closed, at 4:55 p.m. As we walked in, I pulled out my Japanese passport and our American marriage certificate, which recognized our new surname, Matsuo Post, and handed them to a worker, who still seemed enthusiastic to help us even though there were only a few minutes left before the office closed.

"We recently got married in the US and just moved to Japan," I explained. "Well, I'm originally from here, but I've been abroad for a while and just moved back here. Here is a copy of our marriage certificate from California."

The man studied the paper and went to the back of the office to scan our passports.

"First of all, congratulations on your marriage," he said with a genuine smile. I felt a sense of Japanese hospitality. "And second, this document needs to be translated into English. And your wife will need to join your *koseki*. Is your *koseki* still under your family?"

Unmarried Japanese natives have a *koseki*, usually under the name of a parent. Since my wife was not a Japanese citizen, she did not have a *koseki*, and mine was still under my dad's name. Traditionally, it's the husband who holds the main *koseki* in a family.

"What do you mean she needs to join my *koseki*?" I asked with curiosity. "Does that mean her surname will automatically change to Matsuo?"

"Yes, exactly."

"Well, we'd like to change our last name to Matsuo Post, as you can see on our marriage certificate," I pointed at the bottom of the document. "What do we need to do to make that happen in Japan?"

The man scratched his head and filled the silence with a long pause. "*Chotto omachi kudasai*," he said and ran off to the back. This phrase means "please wait a moment," and is something people say in Japan before checking the accuracy of what they're about to say. In Japan, people seem to hold a very high sense of integrity—they are cautious with every word that comes out of their mouths.

"*Sumimasen* (I'm sorry)," I said and made a small bow as he went to ask his colleague about this unusual request. I felt bad for making him stay past 5 p.m. But I needed this information. A few minutes passed, and he came back looking apologetic that it had taken some time.

"You're going to need to get approval from the family court," he said. "And then bring the document to us. If you get approval, we can process your name change."

Now I was mad. Don't couples go to family court to settle divorces? I shouldn't have been surprised, however. Japan is notorious for bureaucracy. If my wife had wanted to change her last name to mine, the process would have been simple: she would have joined my *koseki*, as most women do. But since I wanted to change my name to hers, it made the process more difficult. Going against tradition is hard.

We left the ward office around 5:30 p.m. and returned to my dad's car, where we saw a parking ticket on the window. It was a no-parking zone, but the sign was covered with tree branches. No name change, and a 20,000-yen (about US$180) parking ticket. What a start to our name-changing journey.

After a few weeks of settling back into my home country, I visited the local family court with a translated copy of my marriage certificate and my passport. An older male worker invited me into his office and asked how he could help.

"I recently got married to an American individual, and we changed our last name when we got married in the US," I started again. "And I'd like to do the same in Japan. I've been told to get approval from the family court."

"Has your wife already changed her name in her passport?" he asked.

"Not yet."

"Then she should do that first before joining your *koseki*," he explained. "Bring a copy of your wife's new passport with a translated copy of your marriage certificate. And then, you can submit a request for approval. In Japan, it's not a common practice to combine two names. If you take your wife's last name after she's legally changed it in her home country, you'll have a better chance of getting your request approved."

I wondered who was involved in these name-changing approval requests and how they determined which ones to approve.

These two names sound ridiculous together; they are probably better off with just going with Sato. Rejected.

I imagined a judge flipping through these requests as people swipe right for their next date on Tinder, or whatever dating app people use these days.

When my wife got home that night, I told her what had happened at the court and explained that I needed her to go to the American embassy to get her passport renewed before I could start my part of the process. The problem was, she had three international trips planned in the following two months, and she would need her passport.

After studying how long it could take to renew an American passport, she committed to submitting her passport to the American embassy in Tokyo in November.

A couple of months and three international trips later, my wife submitted her passport renewal application and received it back after two weeks. By this time, it was December, and I headed back to the same family court I had visited several weeks earlier. I was hoping to speak to the same man who had helped me on the previous occasion, but this time I met a different representative.

Once again, I explained my situation and showed him a copy of my *koseki,* my wife's passport with the new last name, and copies of both our original and translated marriage certificates. After carefully studying all the documents, he asked me to fill out an application and then make a copy of my wife's passport at the convenience store across the street.

I ran to the shop and returned with two copies of my wife's passport in different sizes, in case the family court only accepted copies in specific paper sizes. My name was called, and this time I spoke to another different person! *How many people work here?* I wondered. Yet again, I explained the situation and presented the documents with a how-about-now face. The man noticed that I had left the "reason for the name change" column blank.

"What is the reason for doing this?" he asked with genuine curiosity.

"Listen, I can tell you why I want to do it if you have time,"

I answered with a forced smile. He paused and waited for me to go on. I was the one who wanted to accelerate the process, so I quickly changed the direction of the conversation. "But at this point, can you just tell me what gives me the highest chance of approval? What have people written in the past?"

The man told me to write, "Because it is convenient to have the same last name as my spouse when traveling and handling everyday situations in general." Duh.

I signed the paper, stamped my *hanko* or personal seal onto the document, and turned in the paperwork. And I asked for the next step.

"Well, this still doesn't guarantee approval," the man insisted. "You need to wait, and you will be notified by mail in the next two to four weeks."

Two weeks passed, and I received a letter from the family court. It said the court had officially approved my name-change request. However, it also asked me to send back the form with my signature. What the heck?

The court informed me that they needed to wait at least another two weeks to ensure no one was against my request. If someone showed up and objected to our name-change, the court could veto the original request. I hoped the ghosts of my ancestors wouldn't arrive to furiously condemn my departure from the single-named traditions of my family. Apparently, it's usually the angry parent who doesn't approve of her or his child's decision to take her husband's name that exercises this power. Fortunately, I don't have angry parents.

I mailed the document back to the family court and waited patiently. Two more weeks passed, and I received another letter, stating that no one had argued with our request, which meant I had the legal right to officially change my name at the ward office.

I biked to the ward office and submitted my application to officially change my name on my *koseki*. The woman told me this would take one week to process. Of course.

By this point, it was already January 2018. A couple of weeks after my previous visit, I had not heard from the ward office, so I decided to walk in and check. My new *koseki* was ready. This was the moment I had been working towards for so long.

This name-changing journey was not over, however. This was only the beginning. Now I needed to change my name on every form of identification I owned. Driver's license, bank account, passport, you name it. The real work was about to start.

On the same day, I headed to the police station near the ward office. I showed my *koseki* to the police officer at the desk and told her I'd like to change my surname on my driver's license. She looked at me, slightly surprised while maintaining professionalism. Perhaps she had not heard of many men making such a request. "Please fill this form out and wait a moment," she said and pointed me to a bench in the center of the room.

"Matsuo Post san," she called my name, sounding confused about what the Post part of my name meant. "Here is your driver's license with an updated name. Have a good day."

One down. Many to go.

The next hurdle was my insurance card. My health insurance was organized through my employer at the time, so I submitted a name-change request to my manager, with a copy of my new *koseki*. The next day, she approved the process, which automatically changed my work email address from "smatsuo" to "smatsuopost" without any notice. Now I needed to let people know that I had a new email address.

A few weeks later, my new insurance card arrived, bearing the name Matsuo Post.

Two down. Several more to go.

It was time to update my passport. Less than two years prior to changing my name, I had renewed my ten-year passport. I secretly really liked the passport photo of me with my hair in a bun, especially since it was professionally taken. With my long hair gone, I was a little hesitant to get my passport renewed, purely for that reason. But hey, hair will grow back, unless I'm bald in 2028.

I checked my calendar for the next available day I could visit the nearest passport office, and realized that I might not get my passport back before leaving for a work trip and mini-vacation in Hong Kong and South Korea in mid-February. And even if I did, I would need to call the airline to change my name on my plane tickets. I decided to wait until I returned from my trip.

A week after I returned to Japan from the Winter Olympic Games in Pyeongchang, South Korea, I visited the passport office with a copy of my *koseki*. The woman at the counter asked for my wife's passport to verify the spelling of "Post." If I did not provide it, the name would be written phonetically as "Posuto" because that's how the Japanese would pronounce it.

I walked back to my apartment, grabbed my wife's passport, and returned to the passport office again. A different woman, who the first worker had informed about my situation, took my application and voided my old passport with a special hole puncher. A bittersweet moment. Then, she handed me a piece of paper stating that my new passport would be ready to pick up the following week.

I went back to the office to collect my passport on March 8, 2018. Coincidentally, it was International Women's Day. From the moment I returned to Japan after living in the US until that moment, I had been struggling with an identity crisis. A man with a Japanese name and looks, but not so Japanese on the inside after living abroad for so long. I didn't know who I was. But on that day, when my last name officially changed to Matsuo Post, I felt that I was finally able to declare who I am.

I felt victorious. The process to claim my new official identity had been unexpectedly long and challenging because it's rare for a Japanese man to take a foreign partner's name in Japan. I had no idea how many hurdles I would need to jump over just to change my name. Who was I kidding? I was back in Japan again.

The first thought that came to my mind was, *Is this what society expects women to go through if they want to change their last names?* It made me wonder why no one talked about the process. It was just an expectation. This curiosity gave me the motivation to start documenting my feelings and experiences about this name-changing process in Japan.

START WITH WHY

Changing one's last name is a choice, and it's overwhelmingly done by women all over the world. But why? Because our ancestors have been doing it that way for centuries? OK, but why? I can go on and on with these why questions.

Growing up, I thought my future spouse would change her last name to mine. In hindsight, that's only because I had seen my parents and most other married couples in my life do it that way, and I thought that's how I was supposed to live.

While my parents had very open minds about me wanting to study in the US and embraced my choice to marry an American woman, they didn't teach me much about gender equality. My brother is my only sibling, which didn't help me understand girls from a younger age. I was socialized to believe that we are each expected to play our own gender roles. And for a long time, I thought that was normal and didn't know why. I didn't understand why most women took their husband's last name after marriage.

In *Start with Why*, Simon Sinek writes that we need to begin everything with a strong purpose, cause, or belief.[5] I've noticed that my home country, Japan, often doesn't do this well. A woman taking her husband's surname after marriage is one example. In most legal documents,

5 Simon Sinek, *Start with Why* (New York: Portfolio, 2009).

in Japan and many other countries, it's common to ask, "What is your mother's maiden name?" but never the father's.

For the general public in Japan, starting with *why* is a relatively new concept. The norm is starting with *what.* Starting with *what* creates rules, restrictions, and blame. We can always fall back on these norms *because that's how the rules work*. Growing up in Japan, I felt that there were countless unwritten rules in society. I only became fully aware of them when I started living outside the country. Being curious was challenging, yet I persisted. I was always asking my parents, my brother, and myself *why* things were the way they were. I wanted to know *why* certain rules existed and traditions carried on for many years.

I wanted to know *why* I existed.

My journey to feminism has helped me to understand my *why* in life. Even though both my wife and I changed our birth names, I didn't think about having a different last name until I met her. As I delved into feminism, it became clear to me what I wanted to do with my birth name when I got married. My wife helped me to shape what I believed in and the way I see myself as an individual.

Changing my name was a pivotal moment in my journey to feminism. Before I started this process in Japan, I had no idea it was going to take so long, nor how much time and effort I needed to put in. *Am I the only one who feels this way?* I kept asking myself throughout the process.

My conclusion is that if no one talks about this openly, it's because, in most cultures, women are expected to change their names. Or perhaps women *have* been talking about it, but society silences them because men don't want to be the ones to go through this work.

This book isn't about how to change your name in Japan and why you should take your wife's name. I know that if all married couples suddenly combine their last names, future generations will have way too many. Imagine if Joseph Gordon-Levitt and his partner, Tasha McCauley, decided to give their children a combined last name, and one of them got married to my child and chose to combine their names. Their last name would be McCauley Gordon-Levitt Matsuo Post. That's absurd. My point is, I hope our children will have the ability to decide what works for them without being influenced by their gender.

Gloria Steinem says that while the media takes racism seriously, they rarely bother to even pretend to view sexism the same way because "anything that affects males is seen as more serious than anything that affects 'only' the female half of the human race."[6]

6 Gloria Steinem, *My Life on the Road* (New York, Random House Trade Paperbacks, 2016).

For me, taking my wife's name was a wake-up call; I woke up to realize that we live in a patriarchal society. I was angry because it took me thirty-two years to clearly understand the existence of male privilege. We men haven't had to choose to change our identities after marriage. We haven't had to file endless paperwork to make the change legal. We have created the systems that have led to unequal treatment of the sexes for centuries.

Privilege was invisible to me because, as a man, I've *always* had it. I was angry because it shouldn't take a man to take his wife's name to understand we live in a social system that is easier for men. My journey to feminism has given me the opportunity to uncover my story and the courage to take action to transform myself into a man that *I* wanted to become.

So, what was this truth? It was that before I took my wife's name, I had no idea how much this world was tilted in men's favor. Male privilege is a real thing.

Now that I found out the truth, I needed to know more. From that point on, I became obsessed about what other social expectations we have in Japan, and what I discovered was astounding.

I opened a can of worms.

CHAPTER 3

AFTER I TOOK HER NAME

"If it is true that men are better than women because they are stronger, why aren't our sumo wrestlers in the government?"

—TOSHIKO KISHIDA

After I took my wife's last name, I started to notice gender bias everywhere I went in Japan. This experience is called the Baader-Meinhof phenomenon—have you ever noticed that when you buy a new car, you suddenly start to see the same car on the streets all the time? Through my name-changing journey, I got a glimpse into a woman's world for the first time in my life. I had been aware of the concept of patriarchy, but it wasn't until I changed my name that I fully realized we live a patriarchal society.

Changing my name led me to another question: if there is gender bias in a once-in-a-lifetime task like changing names, what do we find in everyday living?

It was a question I didn't want to know the answer to. Maybe I didn't want to know the truth about my home country because I knew it was going to make me angry. But I couldn't stop. I felt a responsibility to find out more.

As I found out more, I realized that patriarchy isn't just harmful to women; it's also harmful to men.

Let me explain.

SPRING 2018, KYOTO, JAPAN

It was a beautiful spring afternoon in Maizuru, Kyoto. Cherry trees were starting to blossom. After the coldest winter in a few decades, the warmth of the new season brought a sense of hope and liveliness. But for the city's mayor, it was a complete disaster.

On April 4, 2018, the city of Maizuru hosted a sumo wrestling event. Before the matches began, the mayor started to give a speech. But several minutes into his oratory, he suddenly lost consciousness and fell flat on the *dohyo*, the arena where sumo wrestling bouts are held. Several men quickly got up on the *dohyo* to check on him, but none of them seemed to know what to do. They weren't doctors. When two women got up on the ring and started to help him, an announcement came over the loudspeaker.

A male voice echoed around the arena. "Women are not allowed on the *dohyo*. Please get off the *dohyo*. Immediately."

Professional sumo is a male sport that excludes women from competition and ceremonies. Traditionally, women are not allowed to enter or touch the ring, because it is believed that this violates the purity of the *dohyo*, as though women were filthy creatures. Sumo is the national sport of Japan, loved by many locals and tourists. Yet, it is one of the most sexist sports in the world.

The two women who climbed up on the *dohyo* were doctors who intended to save the mayor's life. The announcement went on, but the doctors refused to move. It was more important for them to save another person's life than follow the sport's tradition. Thanks to these capable and agile doctors who were courageous enough to break the rules, the mayor recovered his consciousness.[7]

See? I told you patriarchy is harmful to men. This might be an extreme example, but if the female doctors hadn't

---

7 Sirabee, "大相撲· 旧名女性が降りた土俵に「大量の砂」「めちゃくちゃ失礼」と非難の声, published April 5, 2018, https://sirabee.com/2018/04/05/20161573833/.

ignored the sexist tradition of sumo and rescued him in a timely manner, he could have died.

This type of sexism surfaces when people follow the rules without knowing why they exist. The male announcer who demanded the female doctors get off the ring was merely following the rules. Perhaps he thought it was more important to protect sumo's traditions than to save a person's life. Perhaps he thought there were male doctors at the venue, and they could be the ones to rescue the mayor. Perhaps, in his mind, not asking the women to leave the *dohyo* would have gotten him in more trouble than possibly watching someone die. Whatever his motivation, it was clear that he feared breaking with social norms.

The high number of rules in Japan makes this country exceptionally systematic and organized. On the other hand, many people place too much faith in following the rules because they often disregard why those rules exist in the first place.

Working overtime is a major social issue in Japan, to the extent that Japan even has a word for death from overwork—it's called *karoshi*. At many workplaces, there is enormous pressure to work harder. Often, workers interpret working "hard" as working longer hours instead of working more efficiently. In Japan, more than a quarter of workers consistently clock in more than sixty hours a week. Some regularly work more than one hundred hours of overtime a month.[8] This, coupled with the stress of commuting, overwhelms people so much that many have died from brain and heart failure.

Having worked in Japan for several years, I can say that people's commitment toward work is extraordinary. Many people associate their work with their identity and correlate their success at work with their success as people.

Japan reinforces this type of social pressure by publicly dividing people into two categories: *kachigumi*, or the winning team, and *makegumi*, or the losing team. *Kachigumi* individuals are believed to have respectable jobs, loving families, luxurious cars, and other symbols of success. In the eyes of mainstream society, they live the ideal lifestyle. *Makegumi* individuals, on the other hand, are believed to be without these good things. The Japanese media openly joke about *kachigumi* and *makegumi*, on television and in magazines, creating the impression that being on the losing team in life is a source of shame, and everyone should strive to be on the winning team. For many people in Japan, this creates a tremendous amount of stress.

---

8 Uptin Saiidi, "Japan has some of the longest working hours in the world. It's trying to change," *CNBC*, published June 1, 2018, https://www.cnbc.com/2018/06/01/japan-has-some-of-the-longest-working-hours-in-the-world-its-trying-to-change.html.

Rigid social expectations and rules are stressful, and the name-changing process in Japan is no exception. From changing my name in Japan, I learned that this process follows a series of strict, time-consuming rules, especially for a Japanese national who has married a foreigner, because traditionalists don't want to make it easy, thus reinforcing discriminatory practices. In Japan, as many as 94 percent of married women change their last name.[9] As in most other countries, it is socially *expected* for the wife to change her name after marriage in Japan. On top of that, the country doesn't even allow husbands and wives to maintain separate birth names. One of the spouses *must* take the other spouse's name. In a gender-equal world, that number should be much closer to 50 percent for both sexes.

As I mentioned earlier, Japan is far behind most developed countries when it comes to gender equality. It's not all about who changes the surname after marriage. Gender inequality also shows up in pay, the number of senior leaders in businesses, and the government, and the train system.

According to the Organization for Economic Co-operation and Development (OECD), Japanese women suffer from

9 Toko Shirakawa, "Allow different surnames for married couples," *The Japan Times*, published March 7, 2018, https://www.japantimes.co.jp/opinion/2018/03/07/commentary/japan-commentary/allow-different-surnames-married-couples/#.XVQD1XuRWRs.

the third-highest gender pay gap in the thirty-five-country organization at 25.7 percent.[10] Yumiko Murakami, head of the OECD Tokyo Center, describes her experience working in Japan today as "serving her male counterparts."

Shortly after I picked up my new passport, I visited Osaka for a work trip and spent a morning with my team over brunch. At my table, I had three female team members around me (I worked for a company where women made up 80 percent of the organization). After we placed our order, the waiter brought a tray full of silverware.

Since I was sitting closest to the waiter, I grabbed the tray and started putting out the cutlery for the people around me. Two of the three women stared at me in shock.

"I'm not used to this," said one in a surprised voice. "This doesn't happen often here."

Initially, I didn't understand what she meant. Was she referring to the self-service aspect of the experience, that the waiter just handed out a tray full of silverware to the customers? But I quickly realized that she was shocked I would do what I did as the only man at the table.

"Men in Osaka wouldn't do anything like this," said another,

---

10 "The Pursuit of Gender Equality: An Uphill Battle," OECD, published in 2017, https://www.oecd.org/japan/Gender2017-JPN-en.pdf.

who's married to a man from the area. "They expect to be served by women."

The more I learned about gender equality, the more I started to question chivalry. It is actually sexist. Why are men supposed to be polite to just women? We should be kind to people regardless of sex. Chivalry is not something men do to women. It's a way we interpret our behavior to make us feel better about being nice to women. If chivalry is aimed at only one sex, it should be dead. Men should treat other men kindly, too.

The western world developed the concept of chivalry in the twelfth century because people believed women were weak, obedient, and dependent, and should see these qualities as virtuous. Being polite to those who were inferior was considered chivalrous. In Japan, society has also told people to believe that women should be weak, obedient, and dependent, but men are not expected to display polite gestures to women. Rather, women are encouraged to show that these qualities are virtuous by serving men.

Based on my experience at the restaurant, it seems chivalry probably never even existed in Osaka. I kept wondering if I had witnessed an Osaka phenomenon or one that affected Japan as a whole. It's the latter, but I noticed that people in Osaka are generally more open to sharing their emotions than those in Tokyo.

A few months later, I participated in a three-day personal development course in Hong Kong, with more than one hundred people from all over Asia. One of the other participants was a female manager from Osaka. For one of the activities, in which we wrote on pieces of paper who we thought we were, she and I were in the same group. On one of them, I wrote down "feminist." When it was her turn to read what I wrote, the manager became curious.

"What is a feminist?" she asked.

"It's a person who believes in gender equality," I responded in Japanese. "Like myself."

She nodded slowly as if she had never heard of the concept.

Many Japanese locals never think about the idea of gender equality. Through three separate stints living in Japan, I've realized that most Japanese have accepted gender inequality as part of the culture. It is deeply ingrained in their subconscious minds.

I remember when I was in high school completing an internship, I spent a summer working with my father's colleague in San Diego. We talked about being Japanese in the US and all the challenges we faced as minorities. He quoted a message his aunt told him when he was younger and dealing with racism: "At least you are a man."

I've never met his aunt, but that simple, powerful statement has stuck with me to this day. It demonstrates her perception of gender roles in Japan. I don't know how old she was when she shared the message with her nephew but, where she grew up, a person's value is not determined by factors she or he does not control. We are all born with a gender, race, and sexual orientation, and it is unacceptable to treat anyone unequally due to any of those factors. But the world isn't perfect. Sexism, racism, and other types of discrimination exist all over the world today.

The first step toward ending discrimination is acknowledging that it exists. The next step is educating ourselves about why it exists and what we can do about it.

I know it's uncomfortable to talk about these issues. I practiced avoidance for most of my life because all I wanted to do was to conform, not confront. But I'm tired of living a mediocre life, and I know you are, too. Nothing great happens in the comfort zone.

We all need to talk about and educate ourselves on issues that matter to all of us, regardless of where we live in the world. Since I took my wife's name, I have come to see gender inequality everywhere I look, negatively affecting both women and men. I've reevaluated experiences in my own past in light of my new understanding of feminism.

In the rest of this chapter, I want to share some of these experiences with you.

SEX EDUCATION

During my childhood and adolescence in Japan, sex was always a taboo topic. Sex education in Japan consisted of vague concepts and focused on the sensitivity of our genitalia and reproductive organs. The most concrete thing I remember learning was that I shouldn't kick my friends in the testicles during baseball practice.

While we persist in maintaining ideas of chivalry, we find it incredibly difficult to discuss real issues, such as sex, relationships, and consent. When I was at school, the sex education I received was inadequate and confusing.

I was a rowdy fourth grader who enjoyed running between the desks with my friend Takashi. I liked school, but I liked running and jumping more.

When the bell rang to signal the beginning of a new lesson, I rounded the front of the room, skidded to a halt, and quickly found my seat at the back. Uchida-sensei, a short lady who vaguely resembled my mom, returned to the room. Her black bob, perfectly coiffed, bounced as she stepped in front of us. I giggled quietly and eyed Takashi from across the room. Based on the way her shoulders stiffened and she gazed at the back of the room above our heads instead of looking us in the eyes, we knew something slightly scandalous was coming.

"Class. Today we are going to talk about our bodies."

I shrank in my seat, and my ten-year-old heart picked up its pace. Takashi stopped looking at me and started fiddling with his pencils. The atmosphere in the room quickly changed from joyous abandonment to thick awkwardness.

She continued, "As you grow up, your bodies will begin to change. It will be different for boys and for girls."

The kid in front of me shifted uncomfortably, while the slight girl in the seat next to me froze. No one had ever spoken to us this way. Even Uchida-sensei's cheeks turned slightly pink. She continued staring above our heads as she kept her hands tightly clasped in front of her. It was clear: no one wanted to be here.

"For boys, a white liquid will come out of your penis. Girls will experience bleeding each month. This happens during puberty."

My mind reeled. White for boys and red for girls? What does that mean? Uchida-sensei continued speaking for a few more minutes, but all I could comprehend was the color that would one day be attributed to me and my penis. When? Why? How? I never got answers, at least not at school.

Shortly after this confusing class with Uchida-sensei, I sat with my family, eating dinner and watching a TV segment about American culture. The TV crew surveyed American female teenagers and interviewed them about the contents of their purse. A question popped up on the screen: what is the most common object found in a purse?

The answer: condoms.

Confused, I turned to my mom and, in my innocent ten-year-old voice, asked her, "What's a condom?" Just like Uchida-sensei, her shoulders stiffened, and she didn't make eye contact with me.

"Ask your brother," she replied as she continued to watch the screen.

A quick smile escaped the corner of my fourteen-year-old brother's lips, but he just mumbled something unintelligible and went back to eating. My face heated up and I, too, returned to my plate. I still had no idea what a condom was, but their reactions made it pretty clear that I had made everyone uncomfortable. We ate silently for the rest of dinner.

A few years later, I learned about that "white stuff," about condoms, and about sex, but most of my information came from my male friends. Looking back, I wish I had access to better sex education so the learning could have been less shameful and more normalized.

The movie *Boyhood* contains a scene where Ethan Hawke's character talks comfortably about sex with his teenage daughter and son. Granted, they hadn't seen each other for a long time, so his children may have felt like strangers to him. Regardless, it is refreshing to see a natural conversation about sex and pregnancy between a parent and his teenage children. When I watched that scene, I told myself that when I became a parent, I would talk openly about sex with my children.

In many parts of the world, sex is an important yet very uncomfortable topic. In Japan, it's so uncomfortable that people are actually having very little sex. According to a Japanese survey conducted in 2017, nearly half of heterosexual married couples had not had sex in more than a month and did not expect that to change in the near future.[11]

Japan is often heralded as a sexless culture. It's widely known that Japan's population has been decreasing since

---

11 Asahi Shimbun Digital, "セックスレス夫婦、過去最高の４７・２%," published February 11, 2017, https://www.asahi.com/articles/ASK2C2FH8K2CUBQU004.html.

2007. According to the National Institute of Population and Social Security Research, over 40 percent of youths aged between eighteen and thirty-four have never had sex, and over 60 percent have never had a relationship.[12] A twenty-six-year-old Japanese man, who fits into both of these categories, told a BBC reporter that he and his male friends feel that women are "scary."

"We are afraid of being rejected," he said. "So, we spend time doing hobbies like animation."[13]

This doesn't mean young Japanese men are not sexual. They are just terrified of rejection, so they take care of their sexual needs by using pornography or "soap houses," where one exchanges money for the pleasure of soapy hands.

This trend among young Japanese people contributes to the objectification of women. Every convenience store has a visible heterosexual pornography section, and some of these magazines involve rape fantasies. In erotica, there is a common theme of female resistance followed by male persistence. Eventually, the woman submits. This disturb-

12 Mizuho Aoki, "In sexless Japan, almost half of single young men and women are virgins: survey," *The Japan Times*, published September 16, 2016, https://www.japantimes.co.jp/news/2016/09/16/national/social-issues/sexless-japan-almost-half-young-men-women-virgins-survey/#.XyZZfy2cbfY.

13 BBC News, "Sexless in Japan – BBC News," YouTube, uploaded July 9, 2017, https://www.youtube.com/watch?v=*dHePoMNeWo8*.

ing dynamic is deeply conditioned in many countries, especially in Japan, and it's reinforced by a lack of sex education and the ready availability of pornography. Nowadays, pornography is freely available online. It's common for young men, myself included, to encounter our first sexual experience through pornography.

FRIDAY NIGHT WITH MY HOST MOTHER

SPRING 2001, SAN DIEGO, CALIFORNIA, USA

"Shuhei," she was calling my name as she knocked on the door to my room. "Can I come in?"

At fifteen years old, I had recently moved to San Diego, California, to learn English and become as American as I could. Through my school's homestay agent, I had been placed in a four-bedroom home with a widow in her early forties, who had recently lost her beloved husband. Although I knew she was very sad that she had lost her husband, she welcomed me warmly into her life. I quickly felt at home in a foreign country, and she slowly started to open up to me.

One Friday night, she asked me whether she could have a drink with dinner. Knowing that she was well above the legal drinking age, I didn't understand why she asked that question, although I recalled that she had never previously drunk alcohol in front of me. She opened a bottle of wine and started to drink glass after glass of red wine by herself. As the dinner progressed, she chatted incessantly and quickly became emotional. After dinner, I excused myself to get ready for bed. As I drifted off to sleep, I heard a woman calling my name in my dream.

"Shuhei," she said. "Are you awake?"

And then I heard a knock on my door. It woke me up, and I realized my host mother was calling me.

I looked at the clock. It read 1 a.m.

I opened the door and saw her standing in the doorway with tears streaming down her face. She missed her husband and was so grateful to have me in her home.

"Can I give you a back massage?"

I froze. The cold sweat that broke out over my body told me no, but the crying woman in front of me was terrifying. I felt trapped and didn't know how to decline her request. What would happen if I said no? She asked me to take my shirt off and lay flat on the bed. My heart raced, terrified, as she straddled my back. I realized she wasn't wearing underwear.

At that moment, my mind snapped back to attention. I

told her to stop, and thankfully, she did. Her tears intensified, and she accused me of not caring for her the way she cared for me. Leaving my room, she announced her intention to shoot herself with a gun in her room. I didn't know what to do. I panicked. I tried to calm her down and immediately called my school's agent. At 2 a.m., the agent came and took my host mother to the hospital.

That was the last time I ever saw her. By the time she came back from the hospital, my agent had arranged another host family for me.

It took me years to understand that I was sexually assaulted. For a long time, I didn't share my experience with others. I worried that by revealing my story, I was exposing my then-host mother's vulnerability and, in the process, shaming myself. Regardless of her behavior, I still felt a sense of care toward her. We had built a bond of trust, and by sharing the story, I felt like I was breaking that trust.

Why am I telling you this story? In my journey to take my wife's name, I've worked through this trauma and came to understand what happened. It's now blatantly clear to me why many date rape survivors fail to report their cases to the police or close confidantes. I won't ever compare my experience to a rape victim, but that night, I felt as if *I* were the one doing something wrong. I felt guilty, even though I genuinely wanted to be anywhere but that room. If I felt that way, how do the many women who suffer sexual harassment and date rape feel?

In Japanese, the legal term for date rape is *jun-gokan,* or *quasi*-rape. This name implies that date rape is less serious than rape in other circumstances. Japanese lawmakers believe that when a woman is raped by someone she knows, this is less severe than being raped by a stranger.

Whether conscious or unconscious, rape is having sex with someone without their consent. Calling date rape *quasi*-rape is like drinking diet soda and pretending it's healthy.

What happens when we educate our young men using shame, pornography, and limited sex education? How does this affect their perception of sex? In Japan, many young men come to believe that groping or forcing women to have sex is socially acceptable.

The problem of sexual coercion is so great that, as Japan became one of the first countries to introduce camera-equipped phones to the public in 2000, a major social issue also began to surface. People started using the camera feature on their mobile phones to take up-skirt photos of women and schoolgirls, especially on crowded trains. Since sending photos also became a core feature of modern mobile phones, phone providers took it upon themselves to make sure that all mobile phones with built-in cameras came with shutter sounds that could not be disabled. Nearly two decades after the introduction of mobile phones with built-in cameras, mobile manufacturers still enforce this practice in Japan.

Mobile carriers may intend to prevent offensive behaviors, but they are only covering up a much bigger problem. The effect is similar to someone taking espresso shots every day to keep themselves awake, instead of tackling the underlying issue of lack of sleep. Phones that make shutter sounds don't solve the root problem of people taking inappropriate photos of others, and why.

When I was in Hong Kong, I bought a 2017 iPhone without a built-in shutter sound. Since I returned to Japan, I have often encountered a strange problem: whenever I ask someone to take a photo with my phone, they are unsure whether the camera is working. Some people act as though they don't know that it's only in Japan that phones make a shutter sound when using the camera.

My experience illustrates another problem. People who want to take inappropriate photos can buy phones from other countries. We need to tackle the issue of what motivates the behavior. Unless we change the thought process, the behavior will remain the same.

A CLEAN LANGUAGE

SUMMER 2001, RANCHO SANTA FE, CALIFORNIA, USA

When I first moved to the US in 2001, the first school I attended had a group of international students, including some from Japan. Most of them shared similar experiences in their first year in the country. When I arrived in the US, I committed to learning English as quickly as I could. I figured that if I forced myself to live in an environment where I could only speak English, I could learn quickly. As much as it was difficult for me to stay out of my comfort zone of hanging out with my Japanese and international friends, I made a conscious effort to surround myself with local friends. Although my English was minimal to begin with, people accepted my effort to immerse myself into a local way of speaking.

It all began with "What's up?"

Prior to moving to the US, I walked around town, listening to English conversations on my big yellow Walkman. I read textbooks before going to bed and rewrote the same words over and over again until they were locked in my brain. I learned how to say, "This is a pen," but I never learned "What's up?"

At my new school, the kids threw that phrase around like a basketball at recess. To me, it sounded like, "How are you?"

so whenever someone asked me what was up, I responded by saying, "Good!"

One day during PE, my friend Sam greeted me with a high five and a casual, "What's up?" I slapped his hand, feeling like one of the cool guys, and eagerly cried out, "I'm good!"

Sam immediately put his arm around my shoulder and spoke in a very serious voice. I leaned in to hear him say, "Shuhei, that's not how you're supposed to respond when someone says what's up." The sincerity of his tone and the seriousness in his eyes told me to listen closely to this important cultural lesson. "You're supposed to say, "Not much."

This blew my mind. That day, Sam became my unofficial English sensei for the year.

PE was the only class I took that year where students from different grades enrolled. This also became my favorite class because I got to spend more time with Sam, where I learned practical English. He was a kind boy and seemed to genuinely enjoy teaching me English and American culture. At the same time, he became curious about Japanese culture and language.

"How do you say, 'Hello' in Japanese?" he asked one day.

"*Konnichiwa*," I responded, waving my hand.

"Oh, I knew that one," he said, remembering arguably the most commonly heard Japanese phrase outside of Japan.

That day, we played soccer during our PE class. Sam's team lost the game, and he seemed frustrated by the result.

"Shit, Shuhei!" he said as he kicked the grass in the field.

"How do you say, 'Shit' in Japanese?" he asked.

"*Kuso!*" I responded, imitating Sam's tone.

"*Kuso!!*" he kicked the grass again.

I felt a sense of acceptance because an American friend was curious to learn my mother tongue. At the same time, I felt a sense of guilt for teaching him possibly the most profane word in the language.

A year later, I attended a different school in San Diego. Unlike the previous one, this school had hardly any international students, so I stood out as "the Japanese kid." During my first semester, I joined the cross-country team and befriended the runners. Like Sam, they were eager to learn about Japan. In return, they taught me American culture and English. Every time they taught me new slang, they asked me how I would say it in Japanese. As you can imagine, this quickly turned into learning each other's vulgarities.

Vulgarity is often what foreign speakers learn first when studying a new language. Although I felt guilty at first, I quickly became fascinated by these words, especially the word "fuck." There is no comparable word in Japanese—not even close. To me, it was incredible to describe so many situations with this single word.

In return, I got asked, "How do you say 'fuck' in Japanese?"

"We don't have that word in Japanese," I would respond. "It's the cleanest language in the world."

The *cleanest* language in the world.

That's what I thought about the Japanese language at the time. From the Washlet toilet seats that freshen your genitals to having very few garbage bins in public and keeping the streets spotless, Japan is proud to be recognized as a clean nation. Maybe that translates to the cleanliness of the language, who knows. As I mentioned earlier, the most profane word in Japanese is *kuso,* which translates to "shit."

Perhaps this cleanliness hides other aspects of the Japanese language, and stories that aren't being told. Just as we shrink from sex education in the classroom, so we shrink from vulgarity in the language. For men, and for women, the consequences are severe.

PART II

HER STORY

HOW GENDER INEQUALITY AFFECTS WOMEN

CHAPTER 4

PATRIARCHY

OPPRESSION OF WOMEN

"Freedom cannot be achieved unless the women have been emancipated from all forms of oppression."

—NELSON MANDELA

If a lack of sex education and patriarchal language has a negative impact on men, what does it do to women? If men are trapped in a cage of macho behavior, how does the world look to women?

Ignorance about sex and a belief in the cleanliness of the Japanese language mask deep concerns. While men compete to be macho, women are deeply affected by issues of gender inequality around the world. More and more women are speaking up about their experience of harassment or worse.

The #MeToo movement is a powerful response to issues of coercion and rape. In late 2017, the hashtag spread virally on social media as women spoke out about their experiences of sexual assault and harassment. The #MeToo movement took over the world when nearly ninety women made sexual allegations against former film producer, Harvey Weinstein.[14] Since then, numerous survivors have come out to share their stories of sexual assaults. Many high-profile names from many industries, including films, media, sports, politics, finance, and music, have been accused of assaulting individuals. Needless to say, many of them have lost their jobs and credibility.

While the #MeToo campaign quickly became an international movement, it didn't initially rock Japan. Many people have acknowledged that the issue of sexual misconduct exists but have been slow to follow the mainstream campaign. Journalist Shiori Ito, who is credited with starting the #MeToo movement in Japan, spoke out bravely about her experience of being raped by a high-profile journalist, whom she thought was going to hire her. After she accused a former Washington bureau chief from Tokyo Broadcasting System, one of the major TV networks in Japan, the police told Ito that the case wasn't worth pursuing. Why? Because it happened in a private room, known

14 Sara M. Moniuszko and Cara Kelly, "Harvey Weinstein scandal: A complete list of the 87 accusers," *USA TODAY*, published October 27, 2017, https://www.usatoday.com/story/life/people/2017/10/27/weinstein-scandal-complete-list-accusers/804663001/.

as a black box, and there wasn't enough evidence to support her testimony. The police claimed that convictions are rare and speaking out publicly about sexual violence by a public figure could ruin her future career, along with the lives of her family members.

In 2013, according to the United Nations Office on Drugs and Crime, the number of reported rape cases was 1.1 per 100,000 in Japan and 58.5 per 100,000 in Sweden.[15] This doesn't mean Sweden is the world's capital of rape. It simply means that Sweden has the highest number of rape cases *reported* to the police. From looking at these statistics, one might assume that rape is very rare in Japan. But Ito disagrees. She argues that rape happens in Japan as frequently, but that society makes it extremely difficult for victims to come forward.

"It's not that victims haven't come forward; Japanese society wants them to stay silent," she writes in her book *Black Box*.[16]

In her book, Ito shares her experiences of being groped in Japan. She writes that almost all of her female friends experienced groping regularly by the time they reached

---

15 UNODC, "International Statistics on Crime and Justice," published in 2013, https://www.unodc.org/documents/data-and-analysis/Crime-statistics/International_Statistics_on_Crime_and_Justice.pdf1.

16 Shiori Ito, *Black Box* (Tokyo, Bungeishunju, 2017).

high school. Ito and her friends believe that gropers target girls who are too young to associate the unwanted physical touch with groping, or young women who seem shy and insecure, and therefore less likely to report the wrongdoing. A majority of groping in Japan happens on the train during rush hours. And people still wonder why there are women-only train cars in Japan.

Although more women are speaking out about sexual violence as a consequence of the #MeToo movement, the topic remains taboo in many places. After Ito told her story, she says she received more negative feedback than positive.

The most discouraging comments seemed to come from older women, who have lived in a male-dominated world for decades. Ito told an interviewer that many women and men asserted that she was behaving inappropriately for a rape victim:

> "They felt I wasn't behaving the way a Japanese lady should. I was told it was wrong to have the top button of my shirt undone during the press conference. If I had cried, they would have been more sympathetic. One person found a picture on my former coworker's Instagram page of me smiling two months after the incident and asserted that I couldn't possibly be a genuine victim... It was tough but I couldn't let it defeat me as then I would

have become an example of why people shouldn't speak out about these crimes, and that's the exact opposite of my intention."[17]

I watched numerous online documentaries and videos of Ito's press conferences, TV interviews, and stories. What shocked me was the overwhelming amount of criticism attacking her, mostly written in Japanese. Instead of acknowledging her courage to speak the painful truth in public, many chose to humiliate her anonymously.

During an interview broadcast on BBC Two as part of the documentary, *Japan's Secret Shame,*[18] Mio Sugita, Government Member of Parliament of Liberal Democratic Party of Japan, bashed Ito, saying that it is a woman's responsibility to take care of herself in situations where she is at risk of being raped:

"With this case, there were clear errors on her part as a woman," Sugita told the interviewer. "If you are working as a woman in society, you'll be approached by people you don't like. Being able to properly turn down those advances is one of your skills."

17 Matthew Hernon, "Shiori Ito, the Face of the #MeToo Movement in Japan, Speaks Out," *Tokyo Weekender*, published February 2, 2018, https://www.tokyoweekender.com/2018/02/shiori-ito-face-metoo-movement-japan-speaks/.

18 BBC, "Japan's Secret Shame," *BBC Two*, released August 19, 2019, https://www.bbc.co.uk/programmes/bob8cfcj.

The interviewer asked if she had ever experienced any discrimination or harassment, Sugita smiled as though she couldn't believe what she was being asked.

"Of course, if you live in society, you have tons of it," she said. "That's just how it is."

Acknowledging that discrimination is part of society is the first step toward change, but accepting it ends the movement against it.

We must ask: Knowing that society would never look at her and her family the same way, and feeling the tremendous emotional pain of publicly reliving her traumatic experience, why would Ito have come forward with her allegations if they were untrue?

Hiroko Goto, a law professor at Chiba University, says in *Japan's Secret Shame* that historically, Japanese people do not consider violence against women a serious problem.

"People say, 'Forget about it,' and act like nothing happened," she tells the film crew. "Victims are always told it's *their* fault."

Motoko Rich, Tokyo Bureau Chief of the *New York Times*, says that in Japan, there is a different definition of what rape is. "There still is a sense that it's not criminal unless a stranger is attacking you, and you fight back and are hurt," she says. "If it happens between two people who know each other, it can't possibly be rape. And if there is alcohol involved, that's not really rape either."

Astonishingly, Japan's century-old rape laws make no mention of consent. To prove rape in Japan, it is necessary to show that the assailant used force or intimidation. If a victim doesn't cry out for help, it is assumed she or he consented. But as Ito writes in her book, many victims simply freeze when under attack, as she did. This is one of the reasons that the court initially ruled that it was not a crime and dropped the case.

Defending the verdict, Sugita claimed in the documentary that "To doubt that fairness is to insult Japan's judiciary, and Japan's police are *the best* in the world."

She argued that the accused man received hate mail and calls because of Ito's "false accusations" and that men are the ones who suffer significant damage from rape cases.

Even though the federal court initially dropped the case in July 2016, citing insufficient evidence, Ito continued to challenge the judicial system and sexism in Japan. When the Committee for the Inquest of Prosecution decided not to charge the defendant with incapacitated rape, however, there was no common law basis to overturn their decision.[19]

This didn't stop Ito from seeking justice. She alleged that her case was dropped due to political interference. The accused is regarded as one of Prime Minister Shinzo Abe's closest journalistic confidants. In December 2019, a Tokyo court overturned the original ruling and accepted Ito's account of the incident, noting that her actions following the events were consistent and that she had demonstrated objectively that she had no reason to make false claims about her experience.

"It was a long journey," Ito told the reporters at the entrance to the court, more than three years after the initial case was dropped. "But I believe that such small steps can, too, lead to major changes. I hope (the ruling) will become a milestone in the process toward changes in the penal code."

Ito's courageous move to come out publicly as a rape victim in Japan inspired a society that has long been silent about sexual violence. Her hard-fought battle brought much-needed attention to sexual abuse and sex education. Ito continues to teach university students about consent,

19 Magdalena Osumi, "Japan journalist Shiori Ito awarded ¥3.3 million in damages in high-profile rape case," *The Japan Times*, published December 18, 2019, https://www.japantimes.co.jp/news/2019/12/18/national/crime-legal/japan-journalist-shiori-ito-wins-rape-case/?fbclid=IwAR2JKNsPpJIZDZLVocSaDPDt21O4BoTFpCHECjUN3n3z_tRSpPJUR-B2kZQ#.XqOfjC9h3fZ.

which in my experience, was never taught either at home or in school in Japan.

While the #MeToo movement started as a conversation about sexual harassment in the workplace, it also revealed women's historical lack of power. Identifying individual abusers of power is only the beginning. We need to heal the unhealthy culture that supports harassment. It starts with education. We need better sexual education. We need to become comfortable talking about sex when it matters, so that it doesn't take voices like Ito's sharing their experience with sexual violence to bring important questions of consent into our lives.

GENDER AND LANGUAGE

Is Japanese a clean language, or an unequal language? Looking beneath the surface, I think it's inarguable that gender inequality in Japan is enshrined in its language. As I mentioned earlier, when two heterosexual individuals get married in Japan, the couple needs to belong to just one *koseki*, which is why if both partners are Japanese, a married couple must have the same last name. Most of the time, the wife enters the man's *koseki*. This is called *yome ni iku* (嫁に行く), which means "wife moving into her husband's family."

When talking about their spouses, the Japanese use a

gender-discriminatory set of terms. Perhaps the most gender-equal word for wife is *tsuma* (妻), although some argue that the symbol depicts a woman holding a broom.[20] I've noticed that an overwhelming majority of married men call their wives *yome* (嫁). The symbol depicts a woman and a house. To me, *yome* almost sounds like the husband *owns* his wife, since she's the one who joined her partner's *koseki*.

In the summer of 2018, I shared a train ride outside of Tokyo with a male acquaintance in his forties. He was a very generous, kind person who taught yoga in his community. I noticed, however, that he kept calling his wife *yome*. When he spoke about their upcoming trip to Bali, the tone of his story implied that he would *allow* her to come with him. I've never met his wife, but I wonder from the way he speaks about her whether he believes that their relationship is equal.

In my opinion, the most sexist way to refer to one's wife is *kanai* (家内), which means "inside the house." This term arose because wives traditionally stayed inside and did housework while husbands went out to work. Many Japanese married men, especially older ones, refer to their wives this way.

---

20 Kittredge Cherry, *Womansword: What Japanese Words Say About Women* (Berkeley, Stone Bridge Press, 2016).

Recently, I was at a reception dinner in Mie Prefecture, which is just west of Osaka. At my table sat a middle-aged man from Wakayama, south of Osaka, and a younger woman from Mie, both rural locations in comparison to Tokyo. The man and woman had worked together about a decade previously, and it was their first time connecting since the woman had left that organization. In the interim, the man had become a father to two children, and they spoke at length about parenthood.

"My daughters are so adorable," the man said, showing us a photo of his family. "But I'm hardly ever home, even on weekends, to spend time with them and my *kanai*."

"How does your wife feel about that?" the woman asked.

"She and I had a conversation about that over a few beers the other night," the man responded. "I mean, of course, she wants me to spend more time at home, but if you see this from a logical perspective, I'm not that bad."

"How do you mean?" the woman probed.

"Well, I don't bring any issues home, but I do bring decent money home. I'm nice to her and our kids," the man responded. "It's just that I'm not home very often, and it's working out for us. I think I'm a decent husband."

The man's response indicated to me that he did not value spending time with his family. Like many Japanese men, he upheld his "duty" as a man by being busy while his wife took care of the kids. It's not an uncommon perspective in Japan.

The woman then looked in my direction and asked me a question: "You are married to an American person. Does she ask to spend time with you?"

I noticed that she didn't use any of the Japanese words that are used to refer to "wife." She simply acknowledged that I'm with an individual from the US, which I appreciated. I didn't think this dinner with strangers would lead to a discussion of my values, so I was taken aback by the question.

I shrugged. "For me, it is important to spend time with my partner. We actively make time for ourselves and for each other as much as we can. Being together and supporting each other brings our lives meaning."

If the Japanese language perpetuates a sexist attitude toward women, the imbalance is equally clear in the use of the word "husband." The direct translation of this title is "master." Both *shujin* (主人) and the more old-fashioned *teishu* (亭主) refer to the master of the house. *Otto* (夫), a character showing someone wearing the ornamental hairpin that traditionally signaled coming-of-age for Japanese men, is perhaps the most equal word for husband.[21]

I know many Japanese women who still refer to their husbands as *shujin*. I've even heard my mother call my father that sometimes, at his workplace. When I was young, I didn't understand why she referred to her husband differently in different situations. In hindsight, I think it was because she wanted to play a supporting role in my father's success at work by subtly demonstrating that he was the master at home, too.

In my household, my wife and I consider ourselves the co-masters of our relationship. On paper, however, my wife is the "master" of the house. Fortunately, her employer supports us with housing benefits, for which we are tremendously grateful. In fact, in our *juminhyo*, or registry of residential address, my wife is officially the *setainushi*, or household master.

Recently, my wife visited Chiba, a prefecture east of Tokyo, where not many people speak English, for minor surgery on her foot. When she attended the clinic by herself for a pre-operation checkup, a couple of nurses tried to communicate with her about her prescriptions in Japanese. After many blank stares and confused back-and-forth interactions, the nurse pulled out her smartphone and spoke into

21 Ibid.

the translator. *Goshujin nihongo hanasemasu ka?* The phone delivered an English translation: "Does your master speak Japanese?" My wife knew what the nurse meant and politely responded, "Hai" (yes), but what she really wanted to say was, "I am the master of my own life!"

This is why I'm with her.

According to Kittredge Cherry, author of *Womansword*, the concept of marriage as a *yome* or *kanai* wedded to her "master" irritates some Japanese women. Some feminists have come up with a sexism-free alternative that applies equally to all spouses. They suggest *tsureai* (連れ合い) or life partner, based on an old verb for marrying that means to accompany.[22]

Until I read *Womansword*, I introduced my wife as *tsuma*. I thought it was the most gender-equal way of referring to her. I had never met anyone else who called her or his spouse *tsureai*. Now, when I speak Japanese, I refer to my wife as *tsureai* or partner. At first, those who don't know we are married are unsure about the level of our relationship, since the character is also used to describe "allied" nations. I often get a look that says, "What did you just say?"

Despite this momentary confusion, it's important for me

22 Ibid.

to use language that demonstrates that my wife and I are equal partners in our marriage. Interestingly, most Japanese people are unaware of the different meanings of the titles they choose to call their spouses. Even more interesting is that most have never even contemplated the sexist meanings enshrined within the written symbols. It takes patient education to break trends and shift a culture, particularly when it comes to language.

IS JAPANESE REALLY THE CLEANEST LANGUAGE?

When the movie *Tootsie* (1982) first came out in Japan, the scene where actor Dustin Hoffman utters the ultimate English obscenity, "Fuck you," to enrage his female actor friend before her audition, uses the Japanese subtitle that reads "*Busu*."

But *busu* doesn't mean "fuck you." Cherry explains that *busu* is one of those words that illustrates the major gender inequalities of the Japanese language:

> "These nasty words are parallel only in certain situations because *busu* means a woman with a hideous face. It is one of the worst Japanese insults that can be hurled at a female, though it can also be a tease, possibly even for a boyfriend or a pet. The ugly woman called *busu* in Japan would probably be dismissed as a "dog" by English speakers."[23]

23 Ibid.

Cherry also argues that Japan lacks a ladies-first philosophy, which shows up in language. She writes, "Male characters [symbols] get the leadership positions in almost all such words as *danjo* 男女 (male-female), fufu 夫婦 (husband-wife), and *shijo* 子女 (child-girl; here "child" means "boy")." Cherry adds that several phrases in Japanese also indicate Japan's traditional gentlemen-first philosophy by placing the male character ahead. These include *danson johi* (男尊女卑), which means "males respected, females despised" and *fusho fuzui* (夫唱婦随), which translates to "husband calls, wife follows."

This subtle yet consistent male-first message in Japanese is deeply conditioned by the country's education system. When we take a moment to think about it, however, we realize that there is something unethical about it. Just as the mainstream media reinforces beauty standards for women, so language reinforces the primacy of the masculine. The true meaning of such messages is complex, yet it becomes very clear when we understand the context.

Is Japanese the cleanest language in the world? Maybe on the surface or when considering the number of profane words in the dictionary. But the more we understand the context, the dirtier it seems.

Erin Meyer, author of *The Culture Map*, writes about the differences in how various cultures communicate. One of her major points is that each culture relies on a different level of context during interpersonal interactions. In low-context societies, people focus on the simplicity and clarity of communication. On the other hand, people in high-context societies believe that effective communication is more implicit and layered. Japan is one of the highest context cultures in the world, meaning that the Japanese often withhold words but communicate with body language, facial expressions, and tone of voice.[24] In Japan, we call it *kuuki wo yomu*, which means "reading the air." It's a social skill that people in Japan often discuss. A person's social status is correlated with how well they can read the air.

Here is an example of high-context communication. My father has a mentor whom he respects greatly. This mentor is an American gentleman who lived in Japan for over a decade, so he understands the language and the culture. He is a man of few words. When asked for his viewpoint on various subjects, he likes to say, "Not bad." My father, who has spent all of his life in Japan, believes those two simple words can have drastically different meanings depending on the situation. This is because he is trying to understand the nuances of tone and circumstance. In Japan, this type of communication is common.

The United States, on the other hand, is among the lowest

24 Erin Meyer, *The Culture Map* (New York, PublicAffairs, 2016).

context cultures, meaning that people communicate by speaking more directly. It's a country formed of many different cultures, so effective communication requires people to put their ideas into words so others can clearly understand. It's the opposite of Japan, one of the most homogenous countries in the world.

A classic motto of low-context communication is, "Say what you mean and mean what you say." If someone says, "Not bad," that means they think something is not bad. As Meyer mentions in her book, active listening—asking the speaker to speak as clearly and explicitly as possible, then repeating what's been understood as clearly and explicitly as possible—is a form of low-context communication. Living in two countries at the opposite ends of the contextual communication spectrum, I positioned myself somewhere in the middle. Learning about these different styles of communication has made me aware of the dynamics that occur when Japanese people interact with people from other countries. I've realized that not only does Japan's high-context culture shape human relationships, it also shows up in written language.

Japanese is not the cleanest language. We may not have harsh profanities or expressive expletives like English, but the nuances and subtleties of the patriarchal system are entrenched in the structure and makeup of the way we speak.

PATRIARCHY IN LANGUAGE

When I began writing this book, my wife was studying for a master's degree in English linguistics. For her dissertation, she conducted extensive research on the subject of gender and language. It has now become a major topic of conversation in our lives, inspiring me to reflect on my first language.

How does patriarchy show up in everyday Japanese? While there is only one first-person pronoun for girls and women in Japanese, there are a few different first-person pronouns for boys and men. In childhood, little boys are taught to use the pronoun *boku* to differentiate themselves from girls. As a boy ages, he will begin to use *ore* to refer to himself, as he hears older men utilize this pronoun regularly. *Ore* is the most traditionally masculine and dominant way to say "I" in Japanese. At a young age, boys learn to utilize *ore* to demonstrate power and aggression amongst their social groups.

The most gender-neutral and formal way to say "I" is *watashi*. This can be used by both males and females. For girls and women, however, it is the only personal pronoun option at their disposal throughout their lives. Men can choose to use *watashi* in business settings or when speaking to those who hold more authority. If young boys start calling themselves *watashi*, their friends, teachers, and even parents may assume they are different, perhaps even queer. When used by a child, the pronoun sounds more feminine. Interestingly, in professional and business settings, men are expected to use *watashi*, but we should never use it amongst friends and family.

Until recently, I used to refer to myself as *boku* or *ore*. I felt masculine and thought it was natural for me as a man to use those pronouns. As I spent more time learning about feminism, I started to realize that Japanese, like most other languages, is male-dominant. I came to understand that men have more options to refer to themselves based on social situations.

In 2017, during my name-changing journey, I went cold turkey on the use of both *boku* and *ore*. At first, it was very difficult to break the habit. I had used those words for the first thirty-one years of my life. My tongue was used to saying them. On many occasions, I wondered whether others would perceive me as weak and submissive. But that's exactly why I wanted to challenge the status quo; a gender-neutral language does not make anyone less strong or assertive.

After about a year of implementing this practice into my daily life, I finally became comfortable saying *watashi* in any situation. I found it much more difficult to use *watashi* when speaking to my peers and subordinates at work than with superiors. This is because I felt the need to demonstrate authority when talking to peers and subordinates while I felt naturally submissive when speaking to my manager. I have also caught myself saying *ore* when quoting another man in a conversation. This has begun to feel weird as I haven't spoken the word to refer to myself for some time. Subconsciously, I chose to use the pronoun because I wanted to impersonate the person in the story as accurately as possible. For the most part, I now feel neutral and at peace when I'm speaking in *watashi* to everyone in my life.

Oppression of women is woven into our everyday lives, even via our language. We live in a world of patriarchy, but patriarchy also lives in us through systematic sexism that favors men. As Shirley Chisholm, the first black woman elected to the United States Congress, said, "The emotional, sexual, and psychological stereotyping of females begins when the doctor says: 'It's a girl.'" In other words, the oppression of women begins at birth. Yet, the most obvious and impactful gender inequality may be found in the workplace.

CHAPTER 5

INEQUALITY

WOMEN IN THE WORKPLACE

"I'm not bossy. I'm the boss."

—BEYONCÉ

There's no mistaking the figures. Gender inequality has a massive impact on the capacity of women to support themselves economically.

Before we get into how we got here in the first place, it's important to acknowledge where we are today. Let's examine gender gaps from around the world, so we can understand what's holding women back. Here are some recent data from the World Bank, quoted in Melinda Gates's *The Moment of Lift*:

Hungary

On average, men in managerial positions are paid a third more than women in similar positions, and this does not violate the law. In 113 countries, there are no laws to ensure equal pay for equal work by men and women.

Cameroon

If a wife wants to earn additional income, she has to ask her husband's permission. If he refuses, she has no legal right to work outside the home. In eighteen countries, men can legally prohibit their wives from working.

Sri Lanka

Women can work in a shop only until 10 p.m. In other words, men can and need to work jobs after 10 p.m. Twenty-nine countries restrict the hours women can work.

Russia

There are 456 jobs only men can perform because they are considered too dangerous for women. By law, women in Russia can't become carpenters, professional divers, or ship captains, to name just a few positions. One hundred and four countries have laws that allow only men to perform certain jobs. Similar to Sri Lanka, while this can certainly be understood as sexist, others may view these regulations as measures to protect women. While men are viewed as strong and expendable, perfect for these dangerous jobs, women are viewed as weak and in need of protection.

In 1965, only about one in ten people who enrolled in US medical school were women. A century before that, hardly any medical schools admitted women at all. For gender equality in medicine, the year 2017 was a historic year. According to the Association of American Medical Colleges (AAMC), more women than men enrolled in US medical schools for the first time.[25]

Nonetheless, we still have a long way to go before achieving gender equality in medicine. In the United States, only 15 percent of department chairs are women, and male doctors still dominate top leadership positions.[26] While we have made progress, gender inequality persists in many professions, especially in leadership roles.

So why is it so difficult for women to gain entry into a senior role?

A study by a Nordic researcher, who interviewed twenty female Danish and Swedish managers from three different industries, aged between thirty and sixty-five, states that "There is a need for more sophisticated ways of appreciating the experiences of women in relation to man-

---

25 AAMC, "More Women Than Men Enrolled in U.S. Medical Schools in 2017," published December 17, 2017, https://www.aamc.org/news-insights/press-releases/more-women-men-enrolled-us-medical-schools-2017.

26 Nina F. Schor, "The Decanal Divide: Women in Decanal Roles at U.S. Medical Schools," published in February 2017, https://www.ncbi.nlm.nih.gov/pubmed/28834842.

agement."[27] One of the major constraints on managers is the pressure to prioritize work over family. It's not that many organizations are sexist—capitalism demands the same of both female and male managers.

They are the people who put their organization's needs before their own by traveling frequently, being more available, and working longer hours. Many countries in the world lack daycare facilities for parents, so organizations in those countries expect women to take care of their families, making it more difficult for female managers to stay "in the game."

Often, women in managerial and leadership roles are perceived as aggressive, results-driven, and masculine. To succeed in such roles, women are expected to emphasize traditionally masculine traits, then they are criticized. When they see a woman in charge of a workplace, many people assume that she has chosen her career over family, while men in leadership positions rarely face such prejudice.

How is that fair?

Admittedly, many studies have shown that newborn babies are biologically more dependent on their mothers than

---

27 Yvonne Due Billing, "Are Women in Management Victims of the Phantom of the Male Norm?" published January 20, 2011, https://doi.org/10.1111/j.1468-0432.2010.00546.x.

their fathers. But this should not be the only factor in determining whether a mother will stay home and take care of her baby.

What would our society look like if fathers were *expected* to stay at home and take care of the children while the mothers worked full time?

What would the family dynamics look like if women represented half of all the leadership positions in this world?

I bet more men would be stay-at-home dads to support their working wives. That's equal opportunity.

As Geraldine Ferraro, the first woman to run for the US vice presidency on a major party platform famously said, "Some leaders were born women." If half the population in this world were born women, 50 percent of the leadership roles should be filled by women.

I know. It's easier said than done. In her book *Lean In*, Sheryl Sandberg says that it's harder for women to achieve a successful professional life and a fulfilling personal life because of the fundamental social assumption that they cannot be committed to both their families and careers.

To back up Sandberg's point, only twenty-five S&P 500

CEOs are women, a mere 5 percent.[28] While 45 percent of all S&P 500 company employees are female, women hold about 27 percent of senior executive positions, 21 percent of board seats, and represent 11 percent of top earners.[29] While women continue to outpace men in educational achievement, we still see an enormous gap at the top of any industry.

Because of *the glass ceiling.*

The glass ceiling still exists because many people believe that raising children is a mother's job. Arguably, women's ability to breastfeed makes them a good choice as the primary caregiver to a new baby. But this often leads to women leaving the workforce when they have children. A 2007 survey shows that while men's rates of full-time employment never fell below 91 percent, only 81 percent of women who graduated in the early 2000s and 49 percent of women who graduated in the early 1990s were working full time.[30]

On the other hand, this traditional view of mothers as

---

28 Catalyst, "Women CEOs of the S&P 500," accessed, July 15, 2019, https://www.catalyst.org/research/women-ceos-of-the-sp-500/.

29 Catalyst, "Women in S&P 500 Companies," accessed July 11, 2019, https://www.catalyst.org/research/women-in-sp-500-companies/.

30 Lisa A. Mainiero and Sherry E. Sullivan, "Kaleidoscope Careers: An Alternate Explanation for the 'Opt-Out Revolution," *The Academy of Management Executive (1993-200)* 19, no. 1 (February 2005), 106–23.

the primary caregiver makes it challenging for men to leave the workforce. Fathers who wish to drop out of the workforce to devote themselves to full-time childcare may face extremely negative social pressure. Men who leave work early or take time off to care for their children risk negative consequences ranging from teasing to lower ratings in performance reviews.[31] While the numbers are increasing, as of 2017, only one in five stay-at-home parents were fathers.[32]

If we make it too easy for women to leave the workforce, we make it too difficult for men to do so. But why am I challenging the current system if it's working out just fine for men? Generally, we receive higher pay for being born male. Why aren't I advocating that we keep the current system? We could all play to our traditional "strengths"—men could keep working, using our superior earning power to financially support our families, while women leverage their biological advantages as primary caregivers to stay at home and take care of children. That's how we are created, right? Or is it?

In her book *Counting for Nothing*, Marilyn Waring asserts that the current system stays the way it is because "Men won't easily give up a system in which half the world's

---

31 Sheryl Sandberg, *Lean In* (New York, Knopf, 2013).

32 Aaron Terrazas, "Rising Trend of Stay-at-Home Dads Hits All-Time High," Zillow, published January 7, 2018, https://www.zillow.com/research/stay-at-home-dads-20190/.

population works for next to nothing...[and recognizes that] precisely because that half works for so little, it may have no energy left to fight for anything else."

Now, you may be thinking, "Hold on a second. What do you mean by *giving up* this system? We didn't do anything wrong. We've *earned* this. Why don't we just keep this system as is? It's working just fine for us."

So, let me ask, how is it really working for you?

I'm sure the current system is working fine for many of us, both men and women. But what if you *want* to leave the workforce to take care of your children while your female partner takes on the role of breadwinner?

Regardless of sex, we need to empower individual couples to decide who should care for their children and who takes on the role of provider. This could differ for a second or third child as opposed to a first. The next time a working woman in your life announces her pregnancy, just say, "Congratulations!" and stop there. "What are you going to do about work?" is none of your business. You certainly wouldn't ask a man that, would you?

Here is the thing: if you truly care about achieving freedom from gender expectations, you need to do more of the tasks women have traditionally done, *for next to nothing*.

Which tasks? Domestic ones.

If we don't do our part to take care of the home, we are not respecting our property and our partner. If we don't challenge traditional perceptions about raising children, mothers will continue to be the main caregivers of our babies. I don't have children yet, so I will refrain from espousing parenting advice. However, when I do become a father, I'm committed to spending as much time raising my children as my wife does.

As Sandberg says, "The single most important career decision that a woman makes is whether she will have a life partner and who that partner is."

What kind of a life partner supports his woman to achieve her career ambitions?

A man who believes in feminism.

WOMEN IN LEADERSHIP

What's holding women back?

Well, there is a long list. Let's start with educational institutions.

In 2018, *The Japan Times* published a front-page article

exposing Tokyo Medical University for deducting points from the entrance exams of all female applicants, with the intention of keeping the percentage of women studying at the university at about 30 percent. Further, the investigation found that the university added extra points to the score of every male applicant, excepting men who had already failed the test multiple times. This came after the university was caught accepting bribes to boost the scores of children of prominent figures, granting them admission even if they didn't deserve it. Why did they do this? The school believed that too many women resign or take leave soon after getting married in order to start families and raise children.[33] Might this be true? Sure. But what right does an educational institution have to make this assumption for its female applicants?

What else is holding women back?

After the Tokyo Medical University news broke, the hashtag #私たちは女性差別に怒って良い, which means "it's OK for us to be angry about sexism toward women," trended on Twitter. Japanese women spoke out, sharing their own stories of discrimination and exposing issues that have been swept under the rug in Japan for years.

---

33 Kyodo, "Tokyo Medical University discriminated against female applicants by lowering entrance exam scores: sources," *The Japan Times*, published August 2, 2018, https://www.japantimes.co.jp/news/2018/08/02/national/tokyo-medical-university-discriminated-female-applicants-lowering-entrance-exam-scores-sources/#.XT2PiHuRXfY.

Here are some examples that demonstrate the hurtful truth of sexism in Japan today:

"I was a midwife at an obstetrics and gynecology clinic, and thirty minutes before I was about to take leave for my fourth pregnancy, the director called me in and fired me. He's able to make a living because of women giving birth, and he still treated me that way."

"When I reached my eighth month of pregnancy, my boss called me into the conference room. He said that until I wrote a letter of resignation, I couldn't go home. I kept sitting there while he endlessly hounded me. My physical condition worsened, and I wrote my resignation half in tears. Suddenly, I was jobless. From that day, I became aware of the thinly veiled sexism toward women here, and I lost all hope."

"My parents told me, 'Girls don't need an education.' To prove them wrong, I succeeded in entering the highest-ranked university in Japan. When I applied for jobs, I was told, 'If you were a man, we would have hired you instantly.' My enemy wasn't just my parents. It was society."[34]

As a man, and as a human, I'm disappointed. I'm disappointed to be living in a world that allows this type of

34 Rachel and Jun, "What Japanese women are saying about discrimination in Japan," YouTube, uploaded August 13, 2018, https://www.youtube.com/watch?v=T-HWoLVJdoY.

behavior. I'm disappointed in my fellow men who exercise superiority and authority. I'm disappointed that sexism is still a reality.

Being silent about sexism is as unacceptable as expressly supporting it.

Underrepresentation of women is also evident in organizations and politics. Here are some statistics.

A 2017 study by the Organization for Economic Co-operation and Development (OECD) shows a disconnect between female graduates and female managers in Japan. While 45 percent of Bachelor's degree graduates are women, an astonishingly low 12 percent of women hold managerial positions in the workforce.[35] In Japan, graduation rates are split almost equally between the sexes, yet only about one in nine managers is female. The same study indicates that females represent only 9 percent of the seats in parliament. In the 130-year history of modern Japan, not one prime minister has been female.

The rest of the world isn't all that different from Japan. More than one hundred nations have never elected or appointed a woman to the top job, including Spain, the Netherlands, Egypt, Belgium, Russia, and, of course, the US. Even in Iceland, the world's most gender-equal coun-

35 "The Pursuit of Gender Equality: An Uphill Battle."

try, only two women have taken the lead of the republic as the prime minister, and only one woman has ever held the nation's presidency.

According to UN Women, in 2019, of 157 countries that elect their leaders, only eleven women serve as heads of state. This represents a mere 7.2 percent of the world's elected leaders.[36] If we consider all 193 members of the UN, the number remains at eleven, lowering female representation to only 5.7 percent. The field of politics is dominated overwhelmingly by men. It is a world filled with the traditional traits of masculinity—independence, violence, and assertiveness. Without equal representation in politics, governments will continue to implement laws and design structures that favor men and disenfranchise women. Real gender equality is a prerequisite for optimal and rational policy-making, whether for households, countries, or the international community. We need female voices to change these systems, but that can't happen if women must choose between work and home, between education and motherhood, between a life in politics or a life in the kitchen. We need to intentionally change how the system works.

Gender inequality in the workplace has a major impact

36 UN Women, "Facts and figures: Leadership and political participation," UN Women, last updated in June 2019, https://www.unwomen.org/en/what-we-do/leadership-and-political-participation/facts-and-figures.

on the capacity of women to support themselves economically. A lack of female representation in senior leadership positions means more systems that favor men. Systematic sexism is powerful. It is deeply entrenched in our society. When our systems favor one group over another, we all lose; yes, even men.

PART III

HIS STORY

HOW FEMINISM CAN SAVE MEN

CHAPTER 6

HISTORY: PATH TO PRESENT

"Studying the past helps to understand the present."

—CHINESE PROVERB

What does it mean to be a man?

Before answering one of the toughest questions every man needs to answer in his lifetime, we need to understand how we got to where we are today by exploring the history of the gender equality movement.

Let me start with a story.

SPRING 2019, LONDON, UNITED KINGDOM

"The reason why I'm not with anyone right now is because

men in Italy can't accept the fact that I make more than they do."

I was in London for a leadership workshop, where I had the opportunity to meet two dozen senior leaders from other countries. After the first day of the workshop, we all went out to dinner. On my side of the long table sat people from all over the world—Italy, Germany, the US, Scandinavia, Argentina, and Japan. The director from Argentina, who lived in London, was pregnant with her third child. To her gratitude, both she and her husband worked for companies that supported flexible working schedules. Each week, they managed their schedules so one of them was always home with the kids during the day. "It's important that our children see us both as primary caregivers," she explained while taking a sip of her ice water. She emphasized that this arrangement might not be feasible in their home country of Argentina, where traditional social expectations remain pervasive. "If we were back home, my husband wouldn't have these options. He would need to fight against the pressure to be seen as the sole provider for our family."

That was when the Italian manager jumped in.

"Italy is the same way," she said as she leaned toward us, face drawn and clearly frustrated. "Men in Italy feel the need to be the provider. In every relationship, I have made more money than them, and they can't handle it. I was even asked never to reveal my success, especially to their mothers. Poor boys don't want to be emasculated publicly."

THE TRUE COST OF YOUR EGO

Many men, not only in Italy but around the world, fear the perception of weakness. And this perception is often tied to financial success. How can someone be a true man if he makes less money than the women in his life?

In one of her stand-up routines, comedian Ali Wong describes the sudden increase in her income due to her burgeoning fame. "Now I make a lot more money than my husband," she says in *Hard Knock Life*. "My mom is very concerned that he is going to leave me out of intimidation. I had to explain to her that the only kind of man that would leave a woman who makes more money is the kind of man that doesn't like free money."

Men who feel a need to play the role of the provider value their ego more than the "free" money earned by their partner. It's "free" for the man because it's more money for the household without doing more work. Ironically, many men are obsessed with the idea of passive income. They work extra hard to create additional income streams so that one day they can relax and enjoy life without financial worries. Additional income for a household will provide more security for the family. So, when their female partner brings in a lot of cash, isn't that a win for the household?

Well, ego is a funny thing. Many men believe that we must be the ones to bring home the hard-earned check that provides food and comfort. It gives us a sense of self-worth. It convinces us that the things we're doing are worthy of our time.

This type of mindset generates pressure to work harder in order to earn the status of "breadwinner," which often means more responsibility at work, leading to more stress and potentially to health issues. It's a vicious cycle where no one wins. But if we men can let go of our ego and *encourage* our partners when they earn more money, we can release the pressure to be the sole provider. Female income keeps households and children healthier. Studies have shown that an increase in women's income raises the share of household money spent on education, health, and nutrition while decreasing spending on alcohol and cigarettes. To put it simply, letting go of gender expectations gives us more time and better health to enjoy our lives, by doing what matters for our lives with the "free" money our partners bring in. Who wouldn't want that?

BENEVOLENT SEXISM

When I ask people what attributes make a man, I hear

words like provider, security, and protector. These words may appear positive, but they are actually damaging to both women and men. This is called benevolent sexism.[37] Men who feel the need to protect and provide for their partner will likely struggle if their partner earns more money than them or is physically stronger. Benevolent sexism also negatively impacts women. A 2015 study shows that women who supported benevolent sexist views experienced lower relationship satisfaction and confidence, along with higher levels of depression.[38]

If endorsing conventional gender expectations is likely to make both women and men feel unsatisfied, why do we still play those gender roles? When people are asked this question, most say because *it's always been that way.*

When our behaviors don't fully align with our beliefs, we experience stress. In psychology, this is called cognitive dissonance. And when we can't seem to find the solution to that discomfort, we often blame the past. Most of us play the gender role we think we should perform, because that's how we were raised by our parents, who were raised similarly by *their* parents, and so on. Gender norms are

37 Peter Glick and Susan T. Fiske, "Hostile and Benevolent Sexism," published July 28, 2006, https://onlinelibrary.wiley.com/doi/pdf/10.1111/j.1471-6402.1997.tb00104.x.

38 Bettina J. Casad, Marissa M. Salazar, and Veronica Macina, "The Real Versus the Ideal: Predicting Relationship Satisfaction and Well-Being From Endorsement of Marriage Myths and Benevolent Sexism," published March 26, 2014, https://journals.sagepub.com/doi/pdf/10.1177/0361684314528304.

also shaped by the law at the time, which is often a reflection of our cultural values. The question is, how did this all begin?

CURRENT GENDER GAPS AROUND THE WORLD

The examples described in Chapter 5 illustrate gender bias in the world today. While these laws and social customs still exist to keep women down, no one is lifting up humanity to excellence because men are too busy pushing women down.

Imagine how much more productive this world would become if women could earn as much as men for equal work, and if women could earn additional income whenever they wanted, doing whatever job they chose? Men, how much pressure would that take off your shoulders?

In order to undo social customs that keep the world unequal, we must first find the source of discrimination against women.

HOW IT ALL BEGAN

It's always been that way.

Regardless of the issue, it's easy to blame the past so we don't need to take responsibility for the cause of the pain.

We all know that doesn't move us forward. As Part II of this book explained, laws that discriminate against women exist all over the world. If we create our future only by looking at the past, we won't achieve greatness. No revolutions occurred purely by referencing the past.

The real question regarding gender equality is how the heck did we get here in the first place?

In Jimmy Carter's book *A Call to Action: Women, Religion, Violence, and Power*, the thirty-ninth president of the United States writes that men's false interpretation of religious texts is the source of gender discrimination against women:

> "This system is based on the presumption that men and boys are superior to women and girls, and it is supported by some male religious leaders who distort the Holy Bible, the Koran, and other sacred texts to perpetuate their claim that females are, in some basic ways, inferior to them, unqualified to serve God on equal terms. Many men disagree but remain quiet in order to enjoy the benefits of their dominant status. This false premise provides a justification for sexual discrimination in almost every realm of secular and religious life."[39]

It's important to note that this message comes from a

39 Jimmy Carter, *A Call To Action: Women, Religion, Violence, and Power* (New York, Simon & Schuster, 2014).

former world leader who is a dedicated, lifelong Baptist. Now, I'm not a religious person and don't intend to criticize religions. I believe in freedom of religion, and many wonderful teachings from different religions have shaped who I am today.

Nonetheless, I also believe that male-dominant religion is a major factor in the creation and propagation of laws and customs that oppress women. If our oldest institutions have allowed religious leaders around the world to enforce gender bias over the centuries, it makes confronting perhaps humanity's oldest prejudice that much more difficult.

Women have been speaking out about the inequalities they face in patriarchal societies for centuries. Male dominance was imposed in every area of society—from government, law, to marriage and the home—to ensure women stayed inferior to men in terms of their intellectual, social, and cultural status. Unfortunately, there is little evidence of women challenging patriarchy because men controlled the historical record.[40]

However, the concept of "feminism" did not emerge until 1837, when French philosopher, Charles Fourier, first used the term *féminism*. The use of the term gained currency in the UK and the US, where it was used to describe a movement that aimed to achieve economic, social, and

40 DK, *The Feminism Book: Big Ideas Simply Explained* (2019).

legal equality between the sexes, and end oppression of women by men.

A BRIEF HISTORY OF FEMINISM

Most of us spend a significant amount of time in history classes learning which countries won which wars, but very little time learning about the battles women have fought for their human rights. We are not taught the history of feminism.

So, here is a very brief history of feminism in the United States, which is often divided chronologically into four waves:

- First-wave feminism occurred in the western world during the nineteenth and early twentieth centuries. It arose from the same libertarian principles as the drive to abolish slavery, and its primary focus was for women to gain the right to vote.
- Second-wave feminism began in the United States in the early 1960s and lasted roughly two decades, quickly spreading to the rest of the Western world. It focused mainly on sexuality, reproductive rights, and the wage gap.
- Third-wave feminism, which began in the early 1990s in the United States, embraced individualism and

diversity and sought to redefine what it meant to be a feminist.

- Finally, feminism became reenergized in the second decade of the twenty-first century. Fourth-wave feminism focuses on issues such as sexual abuse and the empowerment of women through the use of social media. In addition to advocating for women, fourth-wave feminists believe that boys and men should have better opportunities to express emotions freely, to present themselves as they want, and to be engaged parents to their children. While younger feminists focus on exposing instances of sexism and sexual abuse on social media, some older women question what feminism should actually mean in the modern age. Some argue that in the twenty-first century, feminism is simply common sense.

WHO RUNS THE WORLD?

Even though feminism has only been publicly active for less than 200 years, feminists in the past have made significant strides toward closing the gap in gender equality in the last two centuries. Unfortunately, we are not where we should be today because our history tells us the world has been run by just one sex.

Men.

What about Cleopatra and Beyoncé? Well, there have been some female rulers in history, but the list is extremely short compared with the list of male rulers.

No matter how many young women and girls Beyoncé inspires to run the world, we will not achieve full equality between genders if half of the population is not on board. Which half?

Men.

I will say it again. If we men don't let go of our egotism, we will not see women running the world. Here's the kicker: women having the equal opportunity to run the world may be the *best* thing in the history of humankind.

WHAT'S IN IT FOR YOU?

Feminism is not simply about achieving equality; it's about breaking the gender expectations that hold both women *and* men back. We are not here to perform our gender roles in this play called society. Our purpose is to live an unscripted life, and the word "live" is a verb. It requires action.

As advocates of fourth-wave feminism explain, gender equality isn't just about the empowerment of women. It is also about providing opportunities for boys and men to show emotions freely as opposed to fulfilling the rigid ideal image of what a man should be in today's world. Perceptions of feminism as man-hating are inaccurate. It's not just a women's issue but a matter of human rights, in which men also have a stake. Feminism is also about redefining manliness and freeing men to let go of the fear of not living up to society's gender expectations.

Traditional stereotypes of masculinity often include words like self-reliance, dominance, and stoicism. Unfortunately, these characteristics are correlated with psychological problems such as depression, increased stress, and substance abuse. In every single country in the world, with the exception of China, men are more likely to commit suicide than women.[41] There is a strong link between masculinity and suicide patterns; the need for power, success, and self-reliance sets men up to believe that they have failed, generating a vicious cycle of pain, for which we don't seek help.[42]

Yet, we men are expected to follow the masculine script written by society at all costs; otherwise, that society will revoke our man card. Research has shown that men who fear showing their emotions also display the most violent

---

41 "Figures and facts about suicide," World Health Organization, published in 1999, https://apps.who.int/iris/bitstream/handle/10665/66097/WHO_MNH_MBD_99.1.pdf?sequence=1.

42 Daniel Coleman and John T. Casey, "The Social Nature of Male Suicide: A New Analytic Model," published Fall 2011, 10.3149/jmh.1003.240.

behavior. Men who identify most strongly with conventional masculine traits struggle more with interpersonal problems in their relationships than those who don't.[43] It's a vicious cycle that keeps many men stressed and unhealthy.

Have you ever wondered why men die sooner than women everywhere in the world?

Why do we need to behave in a certain way only because we are born male? We men have been living with a script that dictates we must act tough, as though stoicism and violence were indicators of power. This is toxic and needs to stop. It's a one-sided view of masculinity that leaves us with extremely fragile egos and disconnects us from others.

It's time for us to detox.

---

43 Liz Plank, *For the Love of Men: A New Vision for Mindful Masculinity* (New York, St. Martin's Press, 2019).

CHAPTER 7

MASCULINITY

MACHO IS TOXIC

"Masculinity is a lot like Fight Club; the first rule is that you don't talk about it."

—LIZ PLANK

"Shu is always calm during tough times."

"Shu's emotions are extremely stable. He isn't easily affected by circumstances, positive or negative."

"Shu is stoic. It's sometimes hard to know what he's thinking."

As a manager, this feedback from my employees used to make me soar. In my mind, stoicism was a strength. Staying cool under heat represented power. Hiding my emotions at work indicated leadership. I was doing everything right. As I have explored my truth, however, I've come to understand that these attributes represent the social conditioning that began at birth. I lived my life carefully balancing the two sides of my emotional scale, making sure neither one ever tipped too far in one direction.

Despite my outward calm, I experienced plenty of internal turmoil. From my teenage years to my early twenties, most of my love interests rejected me. I was the skinny Asian kid who desperately wanted acceptance and love. In high school, I was a two-season sport athlete, but never a basketball or football player. In my early college days, I befriended the guys on the water polo team, and if there is anyone in California who is hotter than a college water polo player, I have yet to find him. It seemed like all of my friends had dates to the formals or plans on a Friday night; I watched MTV and wondered what went wrong.

In my sophomore year of college, I was desperate for answers. How do my friends talk so easily to women? Why can't I seem to hold onto a relationship? I read countless articles on dating, and the one that stuck with me most suggested that male emotions were taboo. It implied that a successful dating relationship depends on the male being unpredictable. Showing too much emotion was a sure-fire way of killing the relationship fast. That was it. I had found my answer, or so I thought.

In my senior year, I put into practice all that I had learned. I remained calm and collected around women. I reflected poise and stoicism while burying my emotions. I got a girlfriend who everyone admired. When she broke up with me four months later, she told me that she couldn't live without her ex-boyfriend, who she said she would love for the rest of her life. At those words, my heart tore in two. A thousand daggers ripped through my soul, and my sense of self deflated. We had only been together four months, one semester, but it had felt like so much more. During that time, I gained the acceptance from others that I so deeply craved. I loved to hear the words, "Shu, your girlfriend is really pretty." Most importantly of all, she thought I was cool. My self-esteem was so deeply tied to her opinion of me that when she broke up with me, the ground beneath me fell away.

"Like a man," I held myself together while she gently broke my heart. I retreated to my room, to the safety of solitude, and let the darkness envelope me. For months, I worked out my emotions by myself. In the beginning, I cried into my pillow. I attempted to write love songs that, in hindsight, featured ridiculously melancholic and melodramatic lyrics. By the end of the following semester, I decided that the last bit of water within me needed to harden into ice. Never again would I open my heart wide enough to get hurt. I would pull out my emotional scale and ensure that it remained perfectly balanced, never revealing too much interest in anyone, including myself.

This led me back to the books. Like a good student, I investigated what the so-called-experts say about women. I bought every book on picking up women by *New York Times* bestselling author Neil Strauss, subscribed to *Maxim*, and read every AskMen.com article I could find. I learned "valuable" lessons; for example, that men's and women's brains are wired differently, and that being a man demands confidence. The information I discovered fed my vulnerable sense of self and helped me further craft the armor of masculinity I carried forward into my twenties.

And it worked.

In my mid-twenties, I experienced success with women as it was outlined in these manuals. I played a game of instant gratification. A game absent of emotions. It was as if I had downloaded a guide to hacking dating and could soar past multiple levels at a time.

Not *showing* emotions to others eventually led to me not *feeling* my emotions. I subconsciously associated emotion with pain, so I forced myself not to acknowledge any emotion. This was problematic; at times I wouldn't even celebrate positive emotions. I was so afraid to feel my emotional scale dip that I chose instead to keep it as level as possible. Interestingly, the more I suppressed my emotions, the easier it was to attract women because I wasn't emotionally invested. The stakes weren't very high, so moving on felt like the chorus of an Ariana Grande song, "Thank U, Next."

Deep down, I knew something was missing: genuine emotional connection. I didn't even know how to connect with my true self. It turned out that it wasn't my heart that was crushed into pieces when I was rejected—it was my ego. Do I regret any of my experiences? No. All of the rejections, all of the breakups, and all of the emotionless relationships led me here. Had any of those relationships actually worked, I never would have met my wife. I never would have pushed myself to be better and to investigate my true self. It's possible I would have lived a life of emptiness.

IDOLIZING THE MACHO

Remember Tyler Durden?

You know, Brad Pitt in *Fight Club*. Yeah, *that* Brad Pitt.

The alpha of all alpha males. A dangerously bold, edgy personality with a body that could rival Adonis. A leader, creator, and commander of the pack. He made his woman scream in bed, smoked cigarettes like he could cure cancer tomorrow, and lived life on his own terms.

Tyler Durden was the ultimate sex symbol. The ultimate man. And the rest of us felt it.

If you are like me, you consider Tyler Durden the sexiest man in film. Sure, he was played by Brad Pitt in his thirties when he was in his physical prime, but it wasn't just the six-pack abs that made many of us drool. It was also his dominant personality that screamed of overflowing testosterone. It was his attitude that said, "I do and get what I want."

I'm not the first man to admit that I had a huge crush on Tyler Durden. No, I *worshiped* him. I wanted those abs—the six-pack with the V. I wanted his wild personality. I wanted to be him.

This character was the epitome of conventional masculinity, otherwise known as hegemonic masculinity. He provided a target for men to strive toward: *never cry, be strong, don't show your feelings, play through the pain, suck it up, win at all costs, don't lose, be aggressive, get rich, and get laid.* We are taught to believe that the life Tyler Durden modeled represents the pinnacle of conventional masculinity.

But when a man's reality doesn't live up to his "ideal" masculine life, he experiences a sense of defeat, a low sense of self-worth, and loneliness. This can turn into what therapists call "covert depression," where men refuse to discuss their issues with professionals. Instead, they try to deal with them on their own; admitting emotional pain clashes with expectations of self-reliance and strength. According to family therapist, Terrence Real, "Many men would rather place themselves at risk than acknowledge distress, either physical or emotional."[44] Margaret Atwood, a novelist who is famous for work such as *The Handmaid's Tale,* was once quoted saying, "Men are afraid that women will laugh at them. Women are afraid that men will kill them."

In an attempt to escape such mental illness, many men turn to substances such as alcohol, sometimes augmented by drugs or violence. I turned to alcohol. The time I most wanted to be like Tyler Durden, I drank more alcohol than I can remember to numb the pain of the gap between my ideal life and reality. Instead of seeking help, I used alcohol to numb my fears that my life was out of my hands. When I felt insecure about my masculinity, I subconsciously self-sabotaged.

On the night before my twenty-seventh birthday, I drank so much that I blacked out on my way home. I woke up on the street. I didn't remember how I got there. In hindsight, I'm surprised I wasn't killed, beaten up, or at least mugged. Needless to say, I had a dreadful birthday puking my guts out the next day, but it could have been much worse.

At the extremes of toxic masculinity, men who don't meet

---

44 Terrance Real, *I Don't Want to Talk About It: Overcoming the Secret Legacy of Male Depression* (New York, Scribner, 1998)

the masculine expectations they create for themselves may embark on mass-shooting rampages. In 2014, Elliot Rodger, a twenty-two-year-old student, killed seven people at the University of California, Santa Barbara. A few hours before the massacre, Rodger posted a video online in which he vowed to "slaughter every single spoiled, stuck-up, blonde slut I see," describing his intention to murder women as a form of retribution for his inability to attract them. "I don't know why you girls have never been attracted to me, but I will punish you all for it. It's an injustice, a crime," he said. "I'll take great pleasure in slaughtering all of you. You will finally see that I am, in truth, the superior one. The true Alpha Male."[45]

This man clearly suffered emotional disturbances, but he used his masculinity to justify his actions. The quest for the status of alpha male can be deadly.

In recent times, masculinity has become a trending topic, and there is ongoing debate over what it should be. Yet, masculinity is something we men rarely talk about, because conventional masculinity tells us that talking about masculinity disqualifies us from becoming the alpha male. We are expected to express our masculinity through how we handle our life, which includes being independent,

---

45 "Retribution," *The New York Times*, YouTube, uploaded May 24, 2014, https://www.nytimes.com/video/us/100000002900707/youtube-video-retribution.html.

competitive, and unemotional, exercising self-control, and...eating meat.

MEN, MASCULINITY, AND MEAT

Research on men, masculinity, and meat shows that people in modern society associate masculinity with a lack of remorse for animal consumption. In other words, while women describe feelings of remorse for eating meat, men defend their right to eat animals based on health, hierarchy, and religion. These men believe that caring for animals is a sign of weakness and femininity.[46] Dr. Hank Rothgerber writes, "Denial of animal suffering is congruent with male norms of stoicism, toughness, and emotional restriction. Masculine men are not supposed to relate to the less fortunate, to display sensitivity or empathy, or to discuss their feelings."[47] Not only does masculinity show up in how we treat ourselves and other people, but also in how we treat and eat animals.

Animals existed on this planet long before we human beings came along. Some ate mostly meat, while others ate plants. Later, we categorized those animals as carnivores and herbivores, respectively. Carnivores hunted and ate

46 Jessica Greenebaum and Brandon Dexter, "Vegan men and hybrid masculinity," *Journal of Gender Studies*, published January 11, 2016, https://www.tandfonline.com/doi/full/10.1080/09589236.2017.1287064.

47 Hank Rothgerber, "Real Men Don't Eat (Vegetable) Quiche: Masculinity and the Justification of Meat Consumption," *Psychology of Men & Masculinity*, published 12, 2012.

other animals. They were considered athletic, lean, and attractive. They *owned* the food chain.

On the other hand, plant-eating animals weren't interested in chasing other animals. Their main purpose in life was to avoid those who wanted to eat them. They were considered lazy, fat, and ugly. They *were owned* by the food chain.

The hunter-gatherer culture developed when humans evolved, as far back as two million years ago.[48] Most hunter-gatherers divided labor by sex; men were the hunters who killed animals for food, while women gathered roots, berries, and other vegetal matter. While both men and women ate both meat and vegetables, masculinity is still associated with meat consumption.

Back to the modern day world. In Japan, it's common to refer to some men as *nikushoku danshi* or carnivores, and others as *soshoku danshi* or herbivores. This concept spread through all sorts of Japanese media in 2008, and the term *soshoku danshi* was even nominated for U-Can's "Buzzword of the Year" in 2009.[49] According to philosopher, Masahiro Morioka, who published an article in

---

48 "Hunter-Gatherers," History.com, last updated August 19, 2019, https://www.history.com/topics/pre-history/hunter-gatherers.

49 Kumiko Endo, "Singlehood in precarious Japan Examining new gender tropes and inter gender communication in a culture of uncertainty," published March 1, 2018, https://doi.org/10.1080/09555803.2018.1441167.

2013 on this national phenomenon,[50] *nikushoku danshi* literally means "meat-eating boys"; they are assertive, confident, and love to chase their sexual target. *Soshoku danshi* literally means "grass-eating boys"; they are shy and lack interest in sex, which equates to a loss of "manliness." In Morioka's words, *soshoku danshi* are "kind and gentle men who, without being bound by manliness, do not pursue romantic relationships voraciously and have no aptitude for being hurt or hurting others." The Japanese government even sees this phenomenon as a possible cause of the decline in the nation's population.

If there was a pyramid for different levels of manliness, just like the food chain pyramid, many would place someone like Tyler Durden, the ultimate *nikushoku danshi*, at its peak. Imagine an Uncle Sam-esque political campaign ad aimed at encouraging men in Japan to reproduce. "I want you to be more manly to save our country." Heck, it could even feature a picture of a shirtless, sweaty Tyler Durden pointing at the viewer.

Of course, photos of a shirtless Brad Pitt, along with other athletes or models with perfect bodies, are actually everywhere in public. They're called marketing.

It's no secret that everyday marketing ads on TV, the inter-

---

50 Masahiro Morioka, "A Phenomenological Study of 'Herbivore Men,'" published September 2013, http://www.lifestudies.org/herbivoremen01.htm.

net, in magazines, newspapers, movies, you name it, can shape our perspectives. For the longest time, powerful, muscular, meat-eating, "manly" men have dominated our ideas about how men should be. "If you want to be desired and accepted, be like this guy," is the message they convey.

But why are such men praised more than others? Why does society value "manliness" in men so much? What does being "manly" mean anyway?

Coming back to the food chain, we live in an interesting era when it comes to diet and masculinity. With the recent rise in vegetarianism and veganism, more people are choosing to avoid meat for various personal reasons. Now celebrities and athletes with six-pack abs claim that they are vegetarian or vegan. Heck, as I write this, even Brad Pitt is apparently a vegan.

However, a 2016 study that conducted four psychological experiments to explore the gendered perceptions of vegans showed that vegan men were perceived as less masculine if they were vegan by choice.[51]

It's a misleading perception. While society's definition of hegemonic masculinity may include competitiveness

---

51 Margaret A. Thomas, "Are vegans the same as vegetarians? The effect of diet on perceptions of masculinity," *Appetite* 97, (February 2016): 79-86, https://doi.org/10.1016/j.appet.2015.11.021.

and physical strength, meat-eating doesn't necessarily correlate with those traits.

Mac Danzig, an American mixed martial artist who competed as a lightweight in the Ultimate Fighting Championship (UFC), has been a full-fledged vegan since 2004.

"Stereotypically speaking, a lot of people think veganism is for some skinny, hippy type of person," comments the muscular athlete with a shredded body in the documentary *Forks Over Knives*. "I'm not necessarily trying to break the stereotype. I just tried the diet for my own personal reasons, and it worked for me."[52]

If a UFC fighter like Danzig can be in peak physical form eating a plant-based diet, meat is not a prerequisite for being a physically strong man. Even the Hollywood action legend, Arnold Schwarzenegger is a strong advocate of veganism.

"I ate a lot of meat. They show these commercials, selling the idea that 'real men eat meat,'" the former bodybuilding champion says. "But you've got to understand it's marketing. It's not based on reality."

Schwarzenegger confronts the stereotypical relationship between men, masculinity, and meat-eating as an

52 *Forks Over Knives*, Netflix (2019).

executive producer of the 2019 documentary, *The Game Changers*, along with top athletes such as Lewis Hamilton, Novak Djokovic, Chris Paul, and martial artist Jackie Chan. The documentary features athletes who perform at the highest level eating a plant-based diet and explains the science behind their success. These athletes claim that they are faster, stronger, and have more endurance than before they stopped consuming animal products.

Is this a fad that developed in recent pop culture? No, it's a lifestyle that has been practiced for thousands of years. Research shows that even the gladiators, the original professional fighters from ancient Rome, were predominantly meat-free.[53]

A plant-based diet also saves the environment. Studies show that animal agriculture has detrimental impacts on our planet in seven ways: emitting greenhouse gasses, wasting water, usages of land, producing waste, polluting oceans, destroying rainforests, killing wildlife and humans. Here are some statistics taken from cowspiracy.com:[54]

53 *The Game Changers*, (Netflix, 2019).

54 Cowspiracy, "The Facts," last accessed August 2, 2020, https://www.cowspiracy.com/facts.

GREENHOUSE GASSES

According to the Livestock, Environmental and Developmental initiative, animal agriculture is responsible for 18 percent of greenhouse gas emissions, more than the combined exhaust from all transportation.[55]

WATER

Five percent of water consumed in the US is by private homes, while 55 percent of water consumed in the US is for animal agriculture.

Animal agriculture is responsible for up to one-third of all freshwater consumption in the world today.

LAND

Livestock or livestock feed occupies one-third of the earth's ice-free land.

Animal agriculture is the leading cause of species extinction, ocean dead zones, water pollution, and habitat destruction.

Every minute, seven million pounds of excrement are produced by animals raised for food in the US.

A farm with 2,500 dairy cows produces the same amount of waste as a city of 411,000 people.

---

55 LEAD, "Livestock's long shadow," published in 2006, http://www.fao.org/3/a0701e/a0701e.pdf.

OCEANS

Three-fourths of the world's fisheries are exploited or depleted,

We could see fishless oceans by 2048.

RAINFORESTS

Animal agriculture is responsible for up to 91 percent of the Amazon's destruction.

The leading causes of rainforest destruction are livestock and feed crops.

Up to 137 plant, animal, and insect species are lost every day due to rainforest destruction.

WILDLIFE

USDA predator killing of wild animals to protect livestock.

Ten thousand years ago, 99 percent of biomass was wild animals. Today, humans and the animals that we raise as food make up 98 percent of the biomass.

HUMANITY

Throughout the world, humans drink 5.2 billion gallons of water and eat twenty-one billion pounds of food each day while cows around the world drink forty-five billion gallons of water and eat 135 billion pounds of food each day.

Worldwide, at least 50 percent of grain is fed to livestock.

Eighty-two percent of starving children live in countries where food is fed to animals, and the animals are eaten by western countries.

Each day, a person who eats a vegan diet saves 1,100 gallons of water, forty-five pounds of grain, thirty square feet of forested land, twenty pounds of CO2 equivalent, and one animal's life.

The list goes on. The quickest way for humans to save the environment and humanity is to not eat meat. You can save the environment and humanity—doesn't that sound heroic? And aren't male heroes the epitome of masculinity?

While the rise of vegetarianism and veganism have provided many health and environmental benefits for humans, many men are hesitant to go meatless for various social reasons. They may feel awkward not eating barbeque or rejecting bacon sandwiches while watching a game at a "boys' gathering." Others might feel the social pressure promoted by fast-food chain advertisements that suggest a sausage and bacon sandwich will enhance their masculinity. "Looked at the horoscopes this morning? Reclaim your manliness."[56] Others simply don't want to proclaim, "I don't eat meat."

There is no denying that more men all over the world are practicing a meatless diet. However, many people still associate meat-eating with manliness. Regardless of their diet, men who are assertive and take the initiative are still considered, by the general public, attractive and desired, thereby increasing their level of "manliness."

Ultimately, however, there is no definitive correlation between masculinity and diet.

MASCULINITY IN BOOKS

Gender assumptions that encourage hemogenic masculinity also appear in books.

I recently read a highly enjoyable book creating a life that we truly desire, written by a *New York Times* bestselling author. The book is about developing a highly effective and productive lifestyle. Ostensibly, it has nothing to do with gender equality. When I read it, I wasn't planning to use it for research purposes, but something caught my eye. I noticed a possible gender assumption. At the end of every

---

56 Look At That Ad, "Marketing Mistake: McDonalds' Sexist Burger," published May 23, 2015, http://lookatthatad.blogspot.com/2015/05/mcdonalds-sexist-burger-marketing-mistake.html#.XrEAky9h3jA.

chapter, the author provides a Comfort Challenge section, to encourage readers to create uncomfortable environments. He writes that "the most important actions are never comfortable," explaining that we need to "develop the uncommon habit of making decisions, both for yourself and for others." In one of his Comfort Challenges, he dares readers to get a phone number from "at least two attractive members of the opposite sex each day." What's interesting for the purposes of *this* book is that he follows up that gender-neutral statement by casually warning female readers, "Girls, this means you're in the game as well."

While this book is probably targeted at men, the author does make a subtle gender-related assumption. Asking attractive members of the opposite sex (or whichever sex one's attracted to) for a phone number has long been considered men's responsibility. Men are conditioned to be assertive and undergo a number of rejections in order to succeed. Women, too, participate in and reinforce this cultural expectation. If men don't ask, will women do it? Society associates risk-taking and handling rejection with masculinity. Many people still believe that taking the first step in romantic relationships is a man's job.

The problem with the traditional view of masculinity illustrated by this expectation is that many boys learn from a young age how to be assertive, tough, and stoic. This message is compounded by children's books, media, and the way their parents speak to them. While we now encourage girls to exhibit both feminine and masculine qualities, we often encourage boys to confine their behavior to a very narrow spectrum.

Until the 1970s, an overwhelming majority of characters in children's books played traditional gender roles. Male characters largely demonstrated power and leadership, while female characters tended to appear in supportive, passive roles. Even though we've seen much progress in recent years, the husband-wife dichotomy persists, as does a strong disparity between males engaging in traditionally masculine activities versus traditionally feminine activities.

Portrayals of female characters span a wider range of identities than those of males. In other words, while we still have a long way to go, we have done a good job of empowering girls to be more independent and encouraging them to choose how they want to behave. However, many people struggle with the idea of inviting boys to express greater vulnerability. No wonder many men feel that they cannot show emotions. They have been expected to demonstrate toughness and emotional reserve since they were boys.

MASCULINITY AND HOMOPHOBIA

Many people assume that boys are emotionally illiterate compared to girls. This is simply not true. Boys are naturally as emotional as girls, if not more so. According to Niobe Way, who interviewed hundreds of American boys throughout their adolescence for her book *Deep Secrets*, "boys valued their male friendships greatly and saw them as essential components to their health, not because their friends were worthy opponents in the competition for manhood but because they were able to share their thoughts and feelings—their deepest secrets—with their friends."[57] However, boys are conditioned from a very young age to be emotionally stoic, aggressive, and invulnerable. They soon internalize these expectations. Way also writes that America has a "hyper" masculine culture—a culture in which heterosexual men do not hold hands, and boys do not share beds unless they are from the same family. Because of this, many boys and men feel that they are unable to form intimate male friendships.

In many countries in Asia, heterosexual men, especially those from rural areas, hold hands, share beds with their friends, and regularly rely on those friends for emotional support. Admittedly, this is not a common practice in Japan, but during a recent trip to Sri Lanka, I saw many men holding hands in public. This is despite the country's

57 Niobe Way, *Deepest Secrets* (Cambridge, Harvard University Press, 2013).

suppression of LGBT rights, a hangover from the colonial era.[58]

As an Asian male who spent most of his adolescence in the US, I echo Way's belief that "it is only in modern America and in countries that are heavily influenced by American culture that boys' emotional and social skills and their intimate same-sex friendships are ignored or dismissed as female, childlike, or gay."[59] Perhaps this is why Asians in these American-influenced countries are often perceived as inherently feminine, and possibly gay. This type of hypermasculine culture supports patriarchy and relies on participants to shame anyone who does not conform.

Homophobia exists because of sexism. A hypermasculine culture degrades gay men because they engage in sexual acts that are culturally assigned to women. In other words, being a woman in a hypermasculine culture is the ultimate insult to a man.

In America, "No homo" has become a common phrase, usually used following one man's expression of love and emotion toward another. Heterosexual men find it difficult to express their emotions in a socially acceptable way, so

---

58 "Sri Lanka: Types of criminalisation," Human Dignity Trust, last accessed August 2, 2020, https://www.humandignitytrust.org/country-profile/sri-lanka/.

59 Niobe Way, *Deepest Secrets.*

this phrase provides a buffer to deflect vulnerable emotions. Emotional expression is associated with femininity, homosexuality, and weakness. We have created a society in which females can and must adopt many masculine qualities in order to be strong and seen; when men adopt feminine qualities, however, they are insulted and seen as beta males.

If women and girls are encouraged to choose who they want to be, we must do the same for our men and boys. If we are raising daughters more like sons, we must also raise sons more like daughters. Let's allow men and boys to remove the mask of hypermasculinity.

MASK OF MASCULINITY

Most men deal with many social insecurities. At a very young age, we learn from media, advertisements, and children's books that possessing certain masculine qualities is a vital part of becoming a man.

Lewis Howes, the author of *The Mask of Masculinity*, writes that men struggle with the masculine image that society has created for us. He argues that men wear many masks—from the stoic to the aggressive to the alpha—to disguise our true feelings. "Almost every man has a story in which he learned through pain, humiliation, or even force, how he does not measure up," Howes writes, "When that happens to him, masks become more than hiding places; they become armor."[60]

Through reflection, it has become blatantly clear to me that I, too, have dealt with and continue to deal with many masks of masculinity.

DISCOVERING MY VULNERABILITY

When I met my wife in 2014, I was at a breaking point. I knew my ego was holding me back from authenticity, but I needed more practice and guidance. From day one, my wife expressed curiosity about my current performance of masculinity. She never judged me, but she challenged the views I had worked for years to perfect. She asked questions and tried to understand my approach to life rather than dismiss our differences. At times, I wondered whether she truly liked me, because her independence and self-confidence set her apart from other women I had known.

In the beginning, I was stunned to learn that she wanted to pay for meals. As we walked home from an evening out, she questioned why I wouldn't let her walk closest to the curb. My studies told me that women would feel safe and appreciated if I took care of them in this way. No one had ever questioned my chivalry. And now she didn't like

60 Lewis Howes, *The Mask of Masculinity* (New York, Rodale Books, 2017).

it? The tricks I had learned weren't working on her, and I was often left confused. "Why is she with me?" I would sometimes wonder. Without my manual, what did I have left to offer?

The mask I had been wearing slowly started to slip. The scale was starting to tip, and with her in my life, I could no longer run from my emotions. The phrase "feel your feelings" became a staple of our conversations. She began to recognize when I shut off emotionally and refused to allow it. My silence and retreat into myself only pushed her to seek out my emotions more. I started taking deep breaths and verbalizing the thoughts I had locked away for so long. Sometimes our dinners lasted far longer than planned simply because she made space for me to reach deep inside and find a way to express myself.

When my grandmother suddenly passed away, she left her parent-teacher conferences at school early to come to my side. When she arrived home, I was sitting on the couch in the dark, red-eyed and weeping. For the rest of the evening, I cried on her shoulder. Then, she asked, "How should we celebrate your grandmother tonight?" We ordered Japanese takeout and ate it while I told stories of my loving, open, and joyous Obaachan.

As our relationship developed, I started to learn what it truly meant to be a man. Often, I stumbled and fell. She too made mistakes. We learned together. Through it all, we worked to craft a relationship as free as possible from gender performance.

According to gender theorist, Judith Butler, gender is performative. It is something people *do* rather than what we innately *are*. A person is not born with a gender identity that conditions them to behave in a certain way. We form a fixed gender identity through repeated behavior.[61] Prior to meeting my wife, I was a prime example of a man performing hegemonic masculinity.

As a man, I was conditioned not to cry in front of people. I didn't know the difference between expressing my emotions and allowing emotions to control my behavior. Feelings are natural. But how we respond to them is a choice. Once I understood and practiced this difference, I felt the freedom that comes with sharing myself vulnerably.

Now, I practice letting go of perfection, ego, and stoicism. When my heart is fully open, people can see my whole self. We, men, have been trained our whole lives to wear a mask of masculinity. The way to learn what lies behind this mask is to discover and share our vulnerability. Vulnerability is courage. It is strength within us.

---

61 Judith Butler, *Gender Trouble* (Abington, Routledge, 2006).

VULNERABILITY: DARING GREATLY

Brené Brown, a shame researcher and the author of *Daring Greatly*, states that men experience shame differently compared to women. "Basically, men live under the pressure of one unrelenting message: Do not be perceived as weak," she writes.[62]

We praise those who fight their fear and take risks. To many men, vulnerability is like jumping off a cliff—the fear comes before the jump, but the exhilaration happens upon hitting the water. It takes courage to make that leap. Why should vulnerability be any different? What if we use a hike, instead of a cliff, as a metaphor? A hike can be physically and emotionally challenging, but the path in front of us signals that others have traversed it before. Although a hike takes effort, we can see that it is safe. Vulnerability is much the same. When we start walking the path, we find others who are willing to support us.

In Japanese, the word vulnerability is often translated as *zeijyakusei,* which literally means "a weak characteristic." Brown's book *Daring Greatly* is titled 本当の勇気は「弱さ」を認めること in Japanese, which translates to, "The real courage is to show your weakness." As Brown writes, interpreting vulnerability as weakness is the main issue. Vulnerability requires us to connect with our emotions and reveal our authentic selves. Demonstrating authenticity

62 Brené Brown, *Daring Greatly* (New York, Avery, 2015).

requires courage and strength. Therefore, vulnerability = authenticity = strength.

Openly showing emotions is often looked down upon, not just in Japan but all over the world. I'm not a fan of the saying "fake it till you make it" because it discredits the authentic self. I prefer the saying, "feel the fear and do it anyway."

Many of us men find it difficult to connect with other men about our fears. We have no problem talking about money, sports, or other surface-level topics, but if we share our emotions, we fear judgment from other men. When it comes to authenticity, we are out of practice, and many of us don't know where or how to begin.

During my journey to feminism and this book-writing process, I have encountered numerous fears:

What will my family think of me as a man who has changed his last name and published a book about it?

What will my friends think of me for announcing that I'm a feminist?

Why would anyone be interested in what I have to say about feminism as a man?

What if no one likes my book?

I'm openly sharing these negative voices that have lived in my head. By holding onto them, I was feeding the monster inside me that told me to give up and stopped my feet from taking their next step. By expressing them, I rob those fears of their power, reassuring myself that I fully own my stories and experiences. Sharing our struggles with others is immensely liberating. It's like jumping off of a cliff or stepping onto that path. It is a sign of courage and strength.

Now I invite you to share your fears with the people in your life. Find a quiet space, meditate, journal. Make room for the voices to reveal themselves in whatever way they can. Listen carefully and take note: what is the monster in your head telling you?

After you start understanding your monster and removing the shackles that control you, don't stop. The work is just beginning, and as Neil Gaiman puts it: "The moment that you feel, just possibly, you are walking down the street naked, exposing too much of your heart and your mind, and what exists on the inside, showing too much of yourself. That is the moment you might be starting to get it right."

THE POWER OF CHOICE

According to Susanne Conrad, Founder of Lightyear Leadership, authentic choice connects to our best self, enabling us to live from responsibility and choice. She draws a clear distinction between listening to our fears reactively and practicing choice-based listening.[63]

Below the line of choice, there is only reaction. In this space exists feelings of guilt, judgment, worry, resentment, doubt, and fear. Above the line of choice, we experience feelings of responsibility, trust, forgiveness, wonder, faith, and love. Which side would you rather spend more time in? This is an internal comparison, not an external one.

Being below the line doesn't make you any less of a person; being above the line doesn't make you better than anyone else.

When I'm below the line of choice, I make excuses and blame others. I feel entitled to more and forget that I already have everything I need in my life. I feel mediocre, as though I'm not being the best person I can possibly be. I don't want mediocrity. You don't either.

The power of choice instantly diminishes mediocrity. Choosing to stay above the line takes a commitment to greatness. Imagine a world where everyone has access to the power of choice. A world that acknowledges our differ-

63 "Lightyear Leadership," last accessed March 30, 2020, https://lightyear.co/power-your-future.

ences and chooses to come together to elevate humanity. What does it feel like?

Our deepest fear isn't that we are unable to shift from below the line of choice to above it. Our deepest fear is that the power of choice is beyond our measure. Humanity can be incredibly powerful when we all live in the state of choice. Together, we achieve greatness when we face our fears and choose to expose our true selves to the world.

The world needs more leaders who stand for greatness and do what's right under any circumstance. We need leaders who embrace authenticity and empower others to live in a state of choice, without discrimination. The issue is not our differences but oversimplification and stereotyping.

Traditionally, oversimplification has been used to limit choices and opportunities for women and girls.[64] When we oversimplify one sex, however, we also limit the choices and opportunities available to the other sex. While not every person is created equal, every person should be allowed equal opportunity to choose who she or he wants to be in this world.

For me, changing my last name was an easy choice. It is my way of assuring myself that I stand for what I believe

---

64 Victoria L. Bergvall and Janet M. Bing, "The question of questions: beyond binary thinking," *Language and Gender: A Reader* (Oxford, Blackwell, 1998).

is right, and hold myself accountable to take action for my belief. It may just be four letters at the end of my birth name, but it means the world to me.

I'm not saying all men should change their last names and all women should keep theirs, nor that couples should necessarily combine their last names. My wife and I are fortunate; our combined names only contain a total of ten letters. We are friends with a Thai-Greek couple, each of whose surnames contain more than ten letters. Combining such long names could be absurd.

Changing names is about having choices—no matter how traditional one's society or family might be, every person should have the choice to change or keep her or his last name after marriage.

Many countries already allow married couples to use different last names or combine theirs. But the statistics show that most cultures around the world still pressure men to keep theirs and women to adopt their husbands' surnames. If our legal system allows us to have choices but culture prevents us from exercising those choices, we need to confront cultural norms. In places like Japan, where the wife and husband are obligated to use the same last name, we must first change the legal system.

This is an important step toward equality. Equality allows

us the freedom to choose a life we truly desire. When everyone is living in choice, we are more connected. Connection unites us and lifts up humanity. It's not about one group winning and others losing. We are all in this together.

As men, we have the choice to join the most important movement of the twenty-first century. It takes real strength to acknowledge the inequalities that exist in every culture and devote ourselves to achieving gender equality.

Are you brave enough to recognize that we are not just part of the problem, but we *are* the problem?

Are you man enough to take this problem to heart and commit to solving it for the women in our lives and for ourselves?

If you want to be part of the solution, words are no longer enough.

Fellas, it's time to speak up *and* take action.

PART IV

OUR STORY

WHAT MEN CAN DO TO BREAK FREE

CHAPTER 8

FEMINISM

CONFRONT EXPECTATIONS

"If you stand for equality, you are a feminist. Sorry to tell you, you are a feminist."

—EMMA WATSON

Here is an old riddle.

A man and his young daughter got into a horrible car accident, leaving the father dead and the girl severely injured.

As she was wheeled into the operating room, the surgeon took one look at the girl and said, in a shocked voice, "I can't operate on this girl. She is my daughter."

So how can this be? If you haven't heard this riddle before, give yourself some time to answer.

If you guessed that the surgeon is the girl's gay, second father, you are partially correct. But did you also guess the surgeon could be the girl's mother? If not, you are part of a surprising majority.

In a 2014 study conducted by psychology professors Mikaela Wapman and Deborah Belle, even university students tended to overlook the possibility that the surgeon was a woman.[65] This type of subconscious bias is alive and well, even in the twenty-first century.

DEFINING FEMINISM

Now, let's talk about the F word.

The F word, feminism, puts a lot of people's backs up. They associate feminism with *strong, forceful, and angry women.* Admittedly, there was a period of my life when I associated the word with such qualities in women. *Feminists don't like men,* I thought for a long time. That's because I didn't fully understand the meaning of the word.

While some feminists may fall into this category, they represent the extreme rather than the majority. Assuming that all feminists are angry is like expecting all Christians

65 Rich Barlow, "BU Research: A Riddle Reveals Depth of Gender Bias," *BU Today*, published January 16, 2014, http://www.bu.edu/articles/2014/bu-research-riddle-reveals-the-depth-of-gender-bias/.

to be pro-life. It's called generalization, and we all know that's the root cause of discrimination.

What does feminism actually mean? According to the dictionary,[66] feminism is:

- The advocacy of women's rights on the basis of the equality of the sexes.
- The theory of the political, economic, and social equality of the sexes.
- The belief that women and men should have equal rights and opportunities.
- The doctrine advocating social, political, and all other rights of women equal to those of men.

In short, ***feminism is the belief that women and men are equal.*** We can all agree that women and men are different in our biological makeup, both externally and internally. We are not the same in many ways. But it's important to understand that sameness is not a prerequisite for equality.

As I mentioned earlier, another major misconception about feminism is that feminist women hate men. There is actually a word for the hatred of males—misandry. If you think that being a feminist equals hating men, it may be because you have been conditioned to think that way.

---

66 "Feminism," Merriam-Webster, last accessed August 2, 2020, https://www.merriam-webster.com/dictionary/feminism.

When the first feminist women began advocating for the equal status of women in the late 1700s, they were primarily asking for rights to own property, to attend college, and to vote. But they were often labeled *anti-family, anti-God, and anti-men.*[67]

How about the people who hold up signs that read, "I don't need feminism?" I don't think they understand the meaning of feminism. One young woman in an online community called *Women Against Feminism* boldly stated, "I don't need feminism because when feminists discriminate against men, they discriminate against people I love and respect."[68] This woman evidently believes that feminism pits women against men. She is confusing feminism with misandry. Another woman against feminism writes, "I don't need feminism because I made my own choice to be a stay-at-home mother, and my working husband should not be harassed." This is a beautiful statement about choice, but it has nothing to do with feminism. Just because a woman is a feminist doesn't mean she can't be a stay-at-home mother. That's like saying, "I don't need vegetarianism because I made my own choice not to eat meat, and my meat-eating partner should not be harassed." We need feminism so that wives and husbands all over

---

67 Sam Killermann, "5 Reasons Why So Many People Believe Feminism Hates Men and Why They're Not True," last accessed August 2, 2020, https://www.itspronouncedmetrosexual.com/2012/12/reasons-people-believe-feminism-hates-men/.

68 *Women Against Feminism,* last accessed August 2, 2020, https://womenagainstfeminism.com.

the world will not be harassed for making a choice to stay home full time.

Feminism is *not* a fight against men. It's about fighting for gender equality. Gender equality is about not allowing your gender to dictate what you do.

For example, contrary to what society may believe, a girl doesn't need to like the color pink to be feminine. Nor does a boy need to like the color blue to be masculine. A woman should have a choice to work or stay at home, and the same goes for a man. A feminist woman doesn't need to dress like she hates men because believing in equality shouldn't affect the way she dresses. ***Our gender shouldn't define who we are or our choices about who we wish to become.***

Chimamanda Ngozi Adichie, author of *We Should All Be Feminists*, says that a woman can be a feminist while wearing high heels and a skirt and loving men:

> "At some point, I was a happy African feminist who did not hate men and who likes lip gloss and who wears high heels for herself but not for men," she writes. "The word 'feminist' is so heavy with baggage. You hate men, you hate bras, you hate African culture, that sort of thing."

In another of Adichie's books, *Dear Ijeawele, or A Femi-*

nist Manifesto in Fifteen Suggestions, she composes an extended letter to her childhood friend, instructing her how to raise her newborn daughter as a feminist. Even though her suggestions are focused on raising a feminist daughter, they certainly apply to raising feminist sons. Adichie makes it clear that women and men are different and we should appreciate those differences, but we are all equal. Drawing a line between differences and equality may be a difficult concept for anti-feminists. So, here is an example from Adichie's book:

> "... every woman should have the choice of keeping her name—but the reality is that there is an overwhelming societal pressure to conform...How many men do you think would be willing to change their names on getting married?...women should not be expected to make marriage-based changes that men are not expected to make. Here is a nifty solution: Each couple that marries should take on an entirely new surname, chosen however they want as long as both agree to it, so that a day after the wedding, both husband and wife can hold hands and joyfully journey off to the municipal offices to change their passports, driver's licenses, signatures, initials, bank accounts, etc."

If I were to summarize this book in a paragraph, this would be it.

The best part of feminism? It's inclusive. It doesn't care who you are. In other words, men are welcome to join this movement.

No, let me rephrase it. ***It is our responsibility as men to promote gender equality.***

If half of the world population doesn't care and act on this issue, how can we expect our society to change? After all, equality is good for everyone.

Let's review what feminism is and isn't.

WHAT FEMINISM IS:	WHAT FEMINISM IS NOT:
Believing in gender equality	Believing women are superior
Believing both women and men are equal	Men hating
Believing feminine is powerful	Believing feminine is negative
For everyone	Just for women or gay men

Admittedly, some feminists argue that men who believe in gender equality should call themselves pro-feminists. They believe that feminism is a women's movement, and men cannot be feminists. While I hear their point, I disagree. I believe this is an issue that significantly impacts men. Yes, feminism is about women's empowerment, but it is also about men's liberation through equality.

Men, if you want to elevate your life to greatness, be a feminist, and act like one.

MEN AND FEMINISM

If only half of the world's population participates in the fight against sexism, we will never solve this issue. Author bell hooks believes that feminism is for everybody, including men:

> "Males of all ages need settings where their resistance to sexism is affirmed and valued. Without males as allies in struggle, the feminist movement will not progress. As it is, we have to do so much work to correct the assumption deeply embedded in the cultural psyche that feminism is anti-male. Feminism is anti-sexism."

If a man believes in feminism, it does not mean he hates his own gender. A man could be a feminist and perfectly comfortable with who he is and how he wants to show up to the world. There are muscular guys out there who believe in gender equality. There are "soft-hearted" men out there who believe in feminism. Gay or straight, trans or cisgender. Sexual orientation and gender identity do not matter. Birthplace and race do not matter. If a man believes in equality between women and men, he is a feminist.

Men who believe in feminism exist. But not all of them

truly represent what feminism actually is. Believe me, I was one of those men who say they believe in equal rights but don't categorize themselves as feminists. I was also one of those guys who says they believe in feminism but makes it all about them by proudly liking the color pink and being able to cook. And finally, I was one of those guys who "mansplained" what they thought feminism was. The worst kind. Don't be one of those guys.

According to feminist writer, Krysti Wilkinson, there are several types of "male feminist," and only one of them truly embodies her ideal of the most powerful type of feminist:

> "These men are few and far between, but they exist...They don't buy into the "that's the way things are" or "boys will be boys" nonsense, and they don't try to force unsustainable change brought about solely because of their male privilege. They desire lasting change brought about by well-respected, well-educated, well-known women. *They* are the helpmates, the maids who do the dirty work in the background, and the stay-at-homers who do hours of unpaid, un-acknowledged labor in the fight for equality. We need them. We need more of them."[69]

Some may argue that becoming less of a man by societal standards is emasculation. Technically, emasculation

---

69 Krysti Wilkinson, "7 Types of Men You'll Meet as a Feminist," published January 19, 2017, http://krystiwilkinson.com/7-types-of-men-youll-meet-as-a-feminist/.

means the removal of the external male sex organs. So, unless men are losing their penis and testicles in the process of becoming feminists, emasculation is not an appropriate word. Alternatively, some people may claim that emasculation refers figuratively to removing internal male qualities. I say nothing is sexier than men who are willing to be the helpmates.

FEMINIST ROLE MODELS

A feminist role model I look up to is the writer Jason Basa Nemec. For the majority of the past five years, since the birth of his first daughter, he has been a stay-at-home dad. When I think about the rare type of "male feminist" mentioned above, he is the guy who comes to my mind. This is how he defines what it means to be a man:

> "Masculinity, to me, is showing strength through empathy, vulnerability, and kindness. To me, empathy means thinking about what other people in your community need. My ideal masculine guy is Mister Rogers. He had the saying, "Look for the helpers." To me, masculinity is being a helper."

In today's society, being a man who models that kind of feminism is not easy, especially if one is surrounded by people who don't believe in feminism. As I covered in chapter 7, one of our biggest fears as men is not being perceived as manly. Inside our heads, we are constantly battling with voices that question the manliness of everything we do: *Is this a manly thing to say? Am I acting manly?*

While confidence is widely considered a positive male characteristic, we are often confused about how to be a *real* man. We men need role models who believe in the best in our own gender.

In early 2019, men's razor and shaving giant Gillette ran a controversial advertisement tackling toxic masculinity. The main message of the 1.5-minute commercial is that the definition of masculinity has changed over the years. The advertisement exposes the harmful attitudes of men in the past before urging us to be better. It features a line of men grilling meat, watching two boys fight each other, and justifying it by saying, "boys will be boys." A boy crying on the shoulder of a woman while other boys run through them, calling him a sissy and a loser. Men in the audience of a live play laugh as they watch a male character pretend to grab a female cleaner's butt while she's dusting a cabinet. These are common male behaviors that have been reinforced by society. They are unacceptable and toxic to men and boys. Gillette encourages men to challenge this toxic representation of masculinity and take action today, "because the boys watching today will be the men of tomorrow."[70]

70 Gillette, "We Believe: The Best Men Can Be," YouTube, uploaded January 13, 2019, https://www.youtube.com/watch?v=koPmuEyP3ao.

Terry Crews, former NFL player and popular actor, artist, and activist, challenges toxic masculinity. In 2017, he boldly shared this experience of being sexually assaulted by a "high-level Hollywood executive." He is one of the first men to come forward in the #MeToo movement.

"Women have been talking about this for thousands of years," he said in an interview with Trevor Noah on The Daily Show in May 2018. "Men have turned off...They have heard it so much and stopped listening...When my story broke, it allowed people to see that their lives got stepped on."[71]

Crews explains that sexual assaults are never about sex. Instead, they are always about power. His story is that his agent in Hollywood allegedly grabbed his genitals, not necessarily for sexual pleasure, but to demonstrate his power over his client. Crews argues that success is the number one enabler of sexual assaults.

"Success is the warmest place to hide," he says. "And everyone feels like, 'How can he do this? He is so successful. It's so counterproductive!' But it's not. The thing is, successful people *know* they can get away with it."

---

71 "Terry Crews – The Resurrection of 'Brooklyn Nine-Nine' & Redefining Masculinity," *The Daily Show with Trevor Noah*, uploaded May 20, 2018, https://www.youtube.com/watch?v=07f1HVFpRPI.

As someone who has been very successful in several careers, Crews knows this is true. He openly shares his experiences of winning his battle with the pornography addiction that affected his life and his marriage. For a long time, he kept his addiction secret and justified it because he had been so successful. But deep within, he knew something was missing. He wanted a deeper, more real connection with his wife. One day, he decided to tell his partner of nearly thirty years about his addiction. What she told him was shocking.

"You know we are done, right? It's over."

This is when Crews decided to change for good. He went to rehabilitation to understand what pornography was doing to him.

"I did not go to rehab to win my wife back," he says. "I went there because I needed to be a better person."[72]

Eventually, he restored enough of his wife's trust that she chose to come back, and he's still working on improving their relationship.

"I didn't tell anybody. It was my secret. Nobody knew," Crews said in a video he posted on Facebook. "And that

---

72 Dr. Phil, "Actor Terry Crews On How An Addiction To Porn Almost Cost Him his Marriage," uploaded March 14, 2018, https://www.youtube.com/watch?v=eiostwoEwOc.

allowed it to grow...By not telling people, it became more powerful. But when you put it out there in the open, just like I'm doing right now, it loses its power."[73]

Crews is strong, caring, and vulnerable. For a long time, it seemed like he was living the macho life every man dreamed about—he played in the NFL, became an actor, wrote a book about manhood, has a loving family, you name it—but his true manliness surfaced when he publicly opened up about his struggle with pornography addiction and sexual assault. He understands that gender equality isn't an issue that can be solved exclusively by women. Men need to actively participate in it, too.

"Men need to hold other men accountable," he says.

We need more role models like Crews and my friend, Jason. It's time for us to take action to redefine how to be real men.

REAL MEN DO YOGA

For the longest time, I thought yoga was for women.

When I joined a yoga-inspired athletic apparel brand in 2015, I regretted not beginning my practice sooner.

---

73 Terry Crews, "Dirty Little Secret," Facebook, uploaded February 12, 2016, https://www.facebook.com/realterrycrews/videos/1083942814959410/.

Throughout a typical workday, we stopped the hustle, stopped the noise, and grounded ourselves in the moment. Whether it was at the start of a meeting, a training session, or just 2 p.m., we breathed together and moved together. I discovered my inner yogi.

Yoga can be physically challenging. Yet I discovered benefits of yoga that went beyond the physical to my mind and spirit. Attend a local yoga class, however, and you will likely see far more women than men. I wonder why more men don't go to yoga classes. If you are straight and single, they are arguably one of the best places to meet women. Many men experience a social stigma around practicing yoga. Unlike many other sports, yoga isn't competitive. There is no opponent to face off against. In the eyes of many men, it can't possibly be a real workout if the numbers on the dumbbells aren't continually increasing. If that's your thinking, you clearly haven't taken a vinyasa level two class complete with flows, balance poses, and inversions.

As an avid runner who has run multiple marathons, I can confidently say yoga has improved my performance tremendously. Since I started practicing yoga, I have shaved more than thirty minutes off my marathon time. It has helped me focus on my breathing and given me the flexibility to avoid injury during and after hard runs. If improving your athletic performance is not enough, research says yoga can also boost your sexual health, too.[74] Increased strength, flexibility, mindfulness, endurance, and sex drive—what more can you ask for in an activity? This is why it's not just for women—more men should do yoga.

What does yoga have to do with sexism?

It all comes back to the issue of social expectations. Men think yoga is for women. But there are a number of case studies showing that yoga and meditation have helped high performing CEOs do their jobs better.[75] As you may guess, most of those CEOs are men—95 percent of Fortune 500 companies had a male CEO in 2018—so yoga and meditation *are* popular among a certain group of men. Am I suggesting that only CEOs are real men? No, far from it. I'm saying that the practice of mindfulness is effective for us all. Yoga is not *for* women. Yoga is not weak. Yoga and meditation are for everyone.

MEN AND MINDFULNESS

More than ever, we need mindfulness. The busyness of life and the stress of balancing work and home schedules

74 Naveed Saleh, "5 exercises scientifically proven to boost libido," published March 4, 2019, https://www.mdlinx.com/article/5-exercises-scientifically-proven-to-boost-libido/lfc-3510.

75 Emma Seppälä, "How Meditation Benefits CEOs," Harvard Business Review, published December 14, 2015, https://hbr.org/2015/12/how-meditation-benefits-ceos.

can leave us feeling that we are barely making it to bed each night.

Take the daily commute. Most of us commute by car or train. I am certainly one of those people. I find rush-hour train rides to work highly stressful. Trains are often delayed, making my arrival at work unpredictable. This leads me to leave home extra early, which often means less sleep, causing me to lose focus. On stressful, packed trains to work, I sometimes miss the opportunity to give up my seat for someone who needs it (if I'm lucky enough to have a seat). Someone might be right in front of me, but I'm too busy thinking about how I'm going to spend my day or feeling entitled to a seat because of the high stress level I choose to accept.

When I take care of myself, with a healthier lifestyle that includes more sleep, a better diet, and more time to meditate and exercise, I'm more aware of the moment. What's my secret? I create "me" time in my morning routine before 8 a.m.

- I get up by 5:30 a.m. using an alarm clock, not my phone. I leave that charging in the living room. I brush my teeth to wake myself up. I don't look at my phone first thing in the morning. This saves me a ton of time I would otherwise use scrolling through social media, checking the news, and responding to messages. No one gets to interrupt my "me" time in the morning.

- I practice ten minutes of meditation to ground myself.
- In my journal, I write five things I'm grateful for and my five most important goals.
- I work on a personal project that is not related to my full-time work, such as writing this book or marathon training. I prioritize this time in the morning, because I know I won't do it without dedicating the time. "When I have time" will never happen unless I make that time.
- I go for a run on the road or practice yoga on the mat to get my blood flowing and clear my head.
- I take a shower, get breakfast started for my wife and me, and get ready for the day. The best part? It's only 8 a.m., and I have a whole day to focus on serving others.

On airplanes, flight attendants instruct us to attach our masks first before helping others. Mindfulness and my morning routines have become my mask. It is only when I nourish my own soul that I can truly look around and see the needs of others. When I'm completely present, I recognize what's missing, what needs fixing, and how I can help.

TWO ACTIONS MEN CAN TAKE TO PROMOTE FEMINISM

In her book *The Moment of Lift*, Melinda Gates writes that empowerment of women is "the most comprehensive, pervasive, high-leverage investment you can make in human beings."[76] By lifting up women, we lift up humanity. When we lift up humanity, both women and men enjoy the benefits that come from gender equality.

So, what exactly can men do to promote feminism?

One of the major measures of gender equality is increased female representation in leadership. When powerful women are less of an exception, it's going to feel normal to see women in leadership roles.

Therefore, one of our goals as men should be supporting the women in our lives to achieve their career ambitions.

Here are two crucial actions men can take to empower women:

1. DO MORE HOUSEWORK

Why: In the movie *The Break-Up,* Jennifer Aniston and Vince Vaughn play a couple. At the beginning of the movie, they are going through a break-up. When Aniston's character, Brooke, asks Vaughn's character, Gary, who is busy playing a video game, to do the dishes with her, he unwillingly agrees. Sensing his lack of unenthusiasm, Brooke tells him to forget it, which confuses him. "You just said you want me to help you do the dishes," he says.

76 Melinda Gates, *The Moment of Lift* (New York, Flatiron Books, 2019).

She responds by exclaiming, "I want you to *want* to do the dishes!" When I first watched this film, I was in my early twenties. I was as confused as Gary. *"He's about to do what she's asking!"* I thought. But as I grew older, I understood why Brooke said what she said. Let's face it; *no one likes to do the dishes.* But it has to get done. My wife and I cook almost daily so that we can save money and, more importantly, control what we eat. We also live in a country where dishwashers are almost nonexistent. Now, unless we want our kitchen to resemble the week-old mound that inhabited my shared college home, we need to do the dishes at least twice a day. What I've noticed is that the more I do the dishes, the happier my wife becomes. And her happiness makes me happier.

Do: Spend more time doing the dishes, the laundry, and whatever housework your home needs. This applies to all men living with a wife, girlfriend, a female friend, a mother, or a sister—hell, even do it for your male roommates. A 2018 study found that sharing responsibility for dishwashing represented the single biggest source of satisfaction for women among all household tasks.[77] My trick is to do something I enjoy while doing the dishes. Maybe it's doing the dishes with my partner. Maybe it's putting my favorite Netflix series on in the background. Maybe

77 Dan Carlson, "Not All Housework is Created Equal: Particular Housework Tasks and Couples' Relationship Quality," CCF, published April 3, 2018, https://contemporaryfamilies.org/houseworkandrelationshipquality/.

it's listening to a podcast, which is my favorite. When I associate housework with a pleasurable activity, it is no longer a boring chore but an investment in a more satisfying relationship. We live in the house together, so we take care of it together. When you do more of this, your partner will have more time to focus on what matters outside of the home.

2. TAKE AN EXTENDED CHILDCARE LEAVE

Why: Men want to take paternity leave. But we perceive a stigma around taking time off to care for our children. It seems that taking paternity leave is just not done. We fear that taking time off will jeopardize our opportunities for career advancement, or even that we may be demoted or fired. In the US, although nine out of ten fathers take *some* time off of work for the birth or adoption of a child, 70 percent take less than ten days of leave.[78] In Japan, 85 percent of men said they wanted to take paternity leave but only 6 percent actually took it in 2018. Of the 6 percent of men who took paternity leave, 75 percent took two weeks or less.[79] Contrary to the Gender Gap Index, Japan has one of the most generous parental leave systems in the world. Both mothers and fathers can take up to one

78 U.S. Department of Labor, "Paternity Leave: Why Parental Leave For Fathers Is So Important For Working Families," https://www.dol.gov/sites/dolgov/files/OASP/legacy/files/PaternityBrief.pdf.

79 "男性の育児休業の取得状況と 取得促進のための取組について," Ministry of Health, Labour and Welfare, accessed September 21, 2020, https://www8.cao.go.jp/shoushi/shoushika/meeting/consortium/04/pdf/houkoku-2.pdf.

year of childcare leave. But the reality is that Japanese society pressures men not to take parental leave. This sends a powerful message to men: childcare is not our job. I recently spoke at an event promoting gender equality and had the pleasure of meeting one of the directors of Fathering Japan, an organization that supports male participation in child-rearing. For each of his three children, he took extended childcare leave. He told me that one of the most effective ways to achieve gender equality is for men to take childcare leave. When men leave the workforce, we will naturally lift up women, providing them with more opportunities to shine professionally. Not only that, but men who take parental leave destigmatize the act for other men, which can create a ripple effect.

Do: As the Danish government would say to men, *Orlov—ta' det som en mand!* which translates to "Paternity leave—take it like a man!" Let go of the belief that your self-worth is tied mainly to your professional success. Our self-worth should be tied to how well we do the unpaid, often underappreciated, but most important work in our lives: raising children for a brighter future.

GENDER EDUCATION

Doing more housework and taking extended paternity leave are big steps toward gender equality. I genuinely believe that if all men whose female partners are career-driven commit to these two actions, we will lift up women and drastically increase the chances of allowing more female leaders to shine.

But not every man is in a position to take drastic steps right now. Perhaps you don't plan on having children. Maybe you live solo right now. What else can you do on a daily basis to lift up women and smash the patriarchy?

We can all challenge the language we hear.

"Ladies, you all can sit on this side if you want," a male executive said during a lunch meeting on a rooftop. "The sun is pretty strong on this side."

It was a sunny autumn day in Tokyo. Beautiful clear blue skies with a slight nip in the air. You might think the man was politely demonstrating his chivalry, inviting the women to warm their gentle bodies in the sun. However, he was doing the opposite; while he *was* working hard to be chivalrous, he was actually offering the women the shade. In Japan, along with many other parts of Asia, lighter skin is considered more beautiful, especially for women. The average SPF of Japanese sunscreen is SPF 50+ and many women wear long sleeves and hats even in the most excruciatingly hot summer weather.

"I'd actually prefer to be in the sun," said one female junior-level employee to the executive. "And why was your offer to move to the shade only for the ladies?"

This one quick exchange revealed a lot about the male executive and the female employee. Although the executive intended to show kindness, he directed his largesse only at one gender, based on the assumption that the women would wish to avoid the sun. The female employee noticed the sexism inherent in his remarks and challenged him. With this single comment, she helped us all take a step back and reevaluate why we say what we say.

Education does not happen only at school; we can educate each other in our everyday lives. If we don't say anything, nothing will change. Failing to challenge gender inequality only slows or stops the process.

Sexism is built into many of our everyday phrases. Therefore, it's important to call out sexist comments to educate others. But how much should we get involved? It might be easy to call out people we are close to, but how about strangers?

Recently, I had an opportunity to represent my employer as one of three judges at a pitch event. The other two judges were male executives from two international companies. We waited in a separate room for the event to begin. The two other men struck up a conversation about their careers and how long they had been with their companies. One had worked for the same employer for many years and had just become the head of his company. He started to share how the culture at the workplace has changed.

"I don't know how to deal with young people these days," he said. "When I was younger, when a boss said to do something, we did it without asking any questions. Lately, our employees challenge us if they don't understand why they are doing certain projects."

"Yes, I know," said the other executive. "When I was younger, my boss would yell at me. That was how feedback was given. Lately, I can't do the same thing because my employees would say that's power harassment."

"We're starting to see more women in managerial positions," the first one continued. "But they are usually different."

"Different in terms of what?" I questioned.

"They are usually single and are really into their career," he responded. "They are kind of weird."

The other executive nodded.

I was taken aback by this exchange. I wasn't expecting this

type of conversation right before a work event. Where was this headed?

That's when the host walked in to let us know that the event was about to begin. The three of us curtailed our conversation, stood up, and walked out of the waiting room as if we all agreed that working women were weird. I didn't say anything. Was it that I didn't have enough time? Was I taken too much by surprise? Was I intimidated by their status and age? Regardless of the reason, the moment passed, and I missed the opportunity for education. I spent the rest of the event running possible responses through my head. I even discussed the experience with my wife when I returned home. I stand for greatness and I missed an opportunity. I won't lie, it's hard, but it's so necessary.

What should we do if we hear people using sexist language, or are tempted to use it ourselves? There is no right answer to these questions, but nothing great happens in the comfort zone. When someone says something sexist, ask what she or he means by that. When you are on the verge of using sexist phrases, take a breath and use alternative ones, even if it's inconvenient. If you say the wrong thing, acknowledge your mistake and learn from it.

Our language choices can have a subtle but troubling impact on how we think and act. When we challenge our thinking by using unconventional language to describe the same phenomena, we invite people to question their regular word choices and the understanding of the world that they reflect.

HERE IS A LIST OF COMMONLY USED SEXIST PHRASES TO AVOID USING AND WHAT YOU SHOULD SAY INSTEAD:

- Be a man/Man up
    - **Why:** This usually refers to showing courage. Courage is not reserved for one particular gender.
    - **Say:** If someone is acting like a baby, tell him to grow up instead.

- Act like a lady
    - **Why:** This usually refers to showing sensitivity, politeness, and class.
    - **Say:** If someone is acting aggressively, tell her to be nice or kind.

- Grow a pair/Don't be a pussy
    - **Why:** American actor and comedian, Betty White, said it the best: "Why do people say 'grow some balls'? Balls are weak and sensitive. If you want to be tough, grow a vagina. Those things can take a pounding."
    - **Say:** It's OK to be sensitive and show your emotions.

- You are bossy
    - **Why:** While this is often considered a compliment to boys and men, it's often an insult to girls and women.

- **Say**: Sheryl Sandberg said it the best: "Next time you are about to call a little girl 'bossy,' say instead: she has executive leadership skills."[80]

- Like a girl
  - **Why**: If you are using this phrase to refer to weakness or incompetence, you know that's sexism.
  - **Say**: Make it a compliment instead, like President Obama did when he celebrated the members of the US women's soccer team for their athleticism: "Playing like a girl means you are a badass."[81]

- Boys will be boys
  - **Why**: Have you ever heard someone say, "girls will be girls?" We use it to give boys and men get-out-of-jail-free cards for irresponsible behavior but we don't do the same for girls and women.
  - **Say**: People are fully responsible for their behaviors.

- He's a stud/She's a slut
  - **Why**: While society condones sexual activity and promiscuity in women, men are expected to be pure and remain virgins until they marry. Wait a minute, how did that sentence make you feel? I intentionally wrote that backward. If you felt something was wrong with the sentence, that's because it's an unacceptable sexual double standard. Men throughout the world are encour-

---

80 Sheryl Sandberg, *Lean In*.

81 Michael McIntee, "Obama: 'Playing Like A Girl Means You're A Badass,'" YouTube, uploaded October 31, 2015, https://www.youtube.com/watch?v=uhdQ3rbvSoo.

aged to be promiscuous as a testament to their manhood, while in some countries women may be killed even upon unfounded suspicion of sexual relations outside of marriage. This is one of the most pervasive double standards in the world.[82]

  - **Say**: Research shows that women and men are equally open to casual sex. It's just that women tend to be much more selective about who they have sex with because of their fear of sexual assaults and judgment.[83] Whom and how often people have sex is none of your business. Just say, "This individual is sexually active."

- No homo
  - **Why:** Men and boys usually say this after disclosing their intimate feelings about their close male friends, to make sure that they aren't sounding gay. Not only is this a homophobic statement, it's also sexist. If you need to make sure other men don't think you are gay, it's because you think exhibiting feminine qualities is degrading.
  - **Say**: Just say how you feel about your best buddy like you mean it. I love you, man.

LET'S REWRITE THE SCRIPT

Speaking of showing my feelings about another man, have you seen the TED Talk by American actor, director, and

---

82 Calerie M. Hudson, Bonnie Ballif-Spanvill, Mary Caprioli, and Chat F. Emmett, *Sex & World Peace* (New York, Columbia University Press, 2014).

83 Andreas M. Baranowski, "Gender Differences and Similarities in Receptivity to Sexual Invitations: Effects of Location and Risk Perception," *Archives of Sexual Behavior*, published April 1, 2015, https://link.springer.com/article/10.1007/s10508-015-0520-6.

filmmaker, Justin Baldoni? Watch the video...but finish this book first.

As Baldoni says in his presentation, most of us men pretend to be the man that we are not.[84] We pretend to be strong when we feel weak, confident when we feel insecure, and tough when we are really hurting. It's exhausting trying to be "man enough" for everyone all the time. At a very young age, we learn what kind of man we are supposed to become. Be accepted by other boys. Reject femininity. Act masculine.

Girls are weak. Boys are strong. Hundreds of millions of girls and boys around the world have received this message both consciously and subconsciously.

This *must* stop.

We need a deep cleanse from all the lies associated with the word "masculinity." We need to look inward to remain connected to the authenticity that makes us mindful men, instead of inadvertently reciting the script of this societal play called "Real Man."

It's time to redefine what it truly means to be a strong human and rewrite the script by changing our mindset.

---

84 Justin Baldoni, "Why I'm done trying to be 'man enough,'" TED, uploaded January 3, 2018, https://www.youtube.com/watch?v=Cetg4gu0oQQ.

CHAPTER 9

MINDSET

BELIEVE THE IMPOSSIBLE

Your beliefs become thoughts.
Your thoughts become your words.
Your words become your actions.
Your actions become your habits.
Your habits become your values.
Your values become your destiny.

—MAHATMA GANDHI

Tall people can't run marathons.

I wish I could tell you where I heard this idea. I can tell you it's something I was taught and believed. I think it came from my dad when he saw all the marathon races I watched on TV while I was growing up. The concept was vague, but it had something to do with burning more energy, running out of gas sooner, and hauling extra weight. At 186cm or six-foot, one inch tall, I was told running marathons was a thing I couldn't or shouldn't do. So, I didn't. For twenty-four years of my life.

As a kid, I was a pretty decent runner. I ran track in middle school and cross-country in high school. But until I was twenty-one, I never attempted to run anything longer than ten kilometers or 6.2 miles. Then, a friend of mine casually asked me if I wanted to join him for a half marathon. I finished the race in pain and thought I would never be able to run a full marathon. Ever.

Tall people are not meant to be endurance runners.

But two years later, I read an article that Ryan Reynolds ran the New York City Marathon in three hours and fifty minutes. *If a six-foot-two Hollywood star who's probably too busy to train can finish a marathon under four hours, what's my excuse?* I signed up for my first marathon.

When I did, my mindset changed. It went from *if* to *how*. *How can I get myself ready to run a full marathon in three months?* I started running every day. Every. Single. Day. No matter how busy I thought I was or how tired I was. I stopped drinking alcohol because it was preventing me from training harder. I stopped watching TV at night so I could rest my body more. During these months, I had a singular focus and adjusted my lifestyle accordingly. My goal became my decision maker.

In November 2009, I shattered one of the biggest myths in my life. I finished my first marathon in three hours and thirty-five minutes. Ten years later, I've run seven marathons, with a personal best of two hours and fifty-five minutes that qualified me for the Boston Marathon.

I am a marathoner. I am a tall, fast marathoner.

The best part about this story isn't that I changed my mindset about becoming a tall, fast endurance runner. It's that I contributed to my dad changing *his* mindset about running a marathon.

As a child, my dad encouraged me to run and taught me how to fly down the path with only a pair of shoes. He is the reason why I love running. In his early days, he was a fast runner. He ran countless 10K races and several half marathons but never full marathons. He didn't believe he had enough stamina to run 42.192 kilometers or 26.2 miles. But after seeing me run multiple marathons, he started to believe he could do it, too.

He ran his first marathon at age sixty-seven.

He loved his experience of doing the "impossible" so much so that he now runs a marathon every year.

A positive, determined mindset can be contagious. For a long time, no one thought it was possible to break the four-minute mile. Experts believed that the human body was simply not capable of such a feat. For years, runners from all over the world tried to break the four-minute mile barrier. In the 1940s, someone came close, clocking in at four minutes and one second.

Roger Bannister was a British middle-distance athlete. As part of his training, he relentlessly visualized running a four-minute mile. On May 6, 1954, he smashed through that seemingly impossible barrier, running a mile in 3:59.4.[85] Even though he had not seen anyone run a four-minute mile, he believed he could do it. His belief created a sense of certainty in his mind and body.

Bannister's feat was a worldwide sensation. He became the first person to do something the world thought was impossible, establishing himself as one of the most famous athletes in history. Strangely, less than a year after Bannister's accomplishment, someone else ran a mile in under four minutes. Then some more people emulated the achievement, and so on. Today, even top-level high school

---

85 "Sir Roger Bannister," Academy of Achievement, last revised July 12, 2018, https://www.achievement.org/achiever/sir-roger-bannister-2/.

runners can run four-minute miles. The current world record, which was set in 1999 by Hicham El Guerrouj of Morocco, is an astonishing 3:43.13.[86]

Seeing is believing. While it took Bannister a tremendous amount of visualization to create a belief within himself that he could achieve the impossible, the runners who followed him had his example to follow.

American visionary, Henry Ford, famously said, "Whether you think you can or you think you can't, you are right." In other words, life is all about mindset.

The only thing that defines what you can become is *you*. No matter what circumstances you grew up in, you can change your belief about anything. I didn't grow up in a particularly gender-equal society. I'm not the first man to admit that I've had sexist thoughts and made sexist comments in the past. I was an "ordinary" man who accepted traditional gender expectations and was living the script. Yet, I was able to change my mindset, educate myself, and grow passionate enough to share my experience with you. The results we achieve are determined by our actions. It is through our actions that our thoughts and beliefs take form.

---

86 "Hicham El Guerrouj," World Athletics, https://www.iaaf.org/athletes/morocco/hicham-el-guerrouj-9824.

For example, say you have a perception that men are superior to women. You see men getting paid more, being physically stronger, and monopolizing leadership positions. You use this trend as evidence for your beliefs, reinforcing them. When you hold a limiting belief, you produce a limiting idea or opinion, and repeatedly reinforce it to yourself, consciously or subconsciously. Those voices in your head eventually show up in your behavior. Your behavior—action or inaction—produces consequences. And then your results confirm your original beliefs, as the following diagram illustrates:

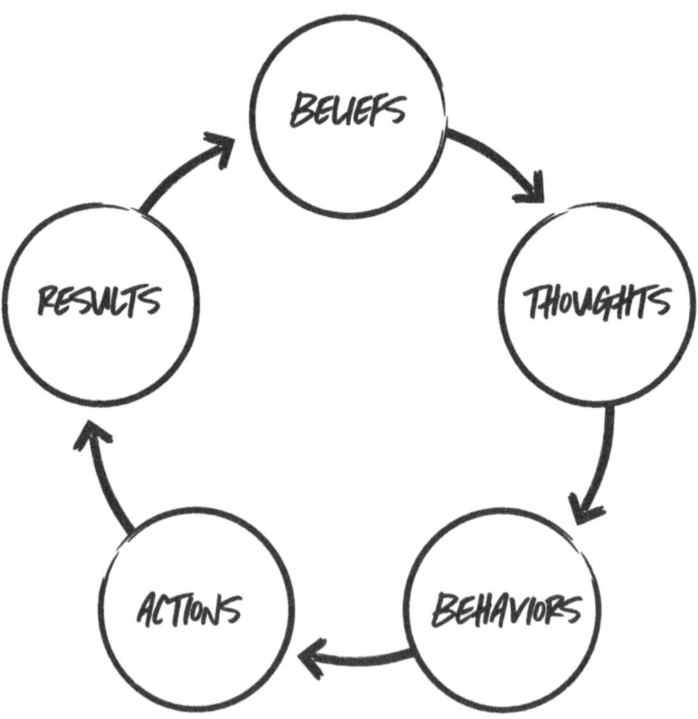

What happens when you replace a limiting belief with a supportive one? A supportive belief is one that supports your moral decisions. It is important to you and aligns with your core values. If you believe that all people are equal, even though you have witnessed and experienced inequality in the past, you will start to visualize an ideal society where everyone is equal. You will start asking yourself, "Our society doesn't yet look like what I truly believe in. What can I do to make a difference?" This will show up in your behavior. You become curious. You ask yourself and others questions. You meet like-minded people. Eventually, you will find some answers to those questions, and those answers will manifest in your actions, producing the desired results. Now you have supported your belief with a result.

Even though external stimulation can impact our cognition, we can learn to control how we interpret our thoughts. Our internal thoughts show up as our behaviors, and consistent behaviors lead to actions, which produce results.

For the first twenty-eight years of my life, I didn't even challenge my beliefs about feminism. I was operating from a limiting mindset. While I acknowledged the existence of gender inequality in the world, I believed that the world was how it was due to our history. I crafted my beliefs only from my personal experiences; what I learned at home, school, and through the media. As Gloria Steinem said,

"The first problem for all of us, men and women, is not to learn, but to unlearn."

Here is an exercise we can practice to unlearn gender. Think of all the gender rules that we have learned in the past. *Men should always pick up the check. Women should clean up the house. Men should always hold the door for women. Women should stay home and take care of children.* Now imagine what it would be like if we assigned roles in relationships based on arbitrary characteristics. The person with the biggest ears should always get the check because the size of ears represents wealth. The person with the thickest hair should always vacuum the floor. The person with the lightest eye color should always hold the door for others. The person with the thinnest lips should stay home and take care of children. How ridiculous would these statements sound? We need to unlearn the arbitrary code that society has given us based on our gender identity.

I am fortunate to have met someone who is a firm believer in feminism, and who is now my lifelong partner. More importantly, she has educated me on what feminism actually means and how it is important to her. This was the external stimulus that led me to alter my beliefs around this topic, which led me to change my name, which led me here.

During my journey to feminism, I have encountered many

challenges: challenges from friends and family, challenges from society, challenges from departments. During my name-changing process, there were times I wanted to give up. Were the months of effort worth it? Giving up would have been so much easier. But it was my strong beliefs and my wife's strong beliefs that motivated me to take action. I kept my focus, developed my mindset, and persisted. Now, when we walk through immigration at an airport, our names are the same—the perfect balance between her identity and mine. It is a new identity that we have created and continue to forge together. Our new family.

What I want you to take away from my stories is not that you need to find a feminist partner or you need to change your surname to change your mindset. It's that you can change your mindset right now. Are you ready?

Take out a pen and paper and answer the questions below honestly:

- What is your mindset toward gender equality and feminism?
- What beliefs do you hold that might be preventing you from expressing what you stand for?
- What thoughts do you hear in your head? Do they support your core values?
- What questions are you asking yourself to achieve gender equality?

- What actions are you committed to taking to make a difference?
- What are the results that you want to see? How will they shape your beliefs?

Albert Einstein said, "The most important decision we make is whether we believe we live in a friendly or hostile universe." If we choose to believe that we live in a friendly universe, we can free ourselves from the imprisonment of limited perception. We will start to see that everything that happens in life has a purpose, even if it's painful at the time. Adversity is an opportunity for our souls to grow. If we encounter discomfort, we can rewrite the script ourselves. We are creating our lives and our belief systems in tandem. We have the power to change what's happening in reality by changing what's happening between our ears.

It all starts with mindset. No matter what upbringing you had or what environment you live in now, if you fundamentally value equality between women and men, you can change your beliefs. As men, it is our responsibility to hold each other accountable for our words and actions. Not doing anything about foul language and actions that push us back from achieving equality only reinforces those behaviors.

This process is not a switch you can turn on or off. Reading this book or doing this mindset exercise once won't change you forever. It's a journey filled with discipline and commitment. But this is our path to freedom. As Eleanor Roosevelt once said, "Freedom makes a huge requirement of every human being. With freedom comes responsibility. For the person who is unwilling to grow up, the person who does not want to carry his own weight, this is a frightening prospect."

Men, are you brave enough to step forward with great intent and still acknowledge that you might be wrong in that intent? Traditionally, we are known as fixers. Our natural inclination is to fix issues in front of us. When we see a problem, we want to solve it, right? Well, there is a massive problem with gender inequality in this world, and we need to *fix* it for humanity—and yes, that includes men. Obviously, we can't do it alone. We need to do this in collaboration with women. First, we need to listen to everyone's experience with this topic. Just listen to understand—nothing more. When we understand different points of view wholeheartedly, we will start to recognize the disconnect and understand how we can bring the genders together.

This is not about branding ourselves so we can be more attractive to women. It's not about always saying the right things or doing the right things. This is about living our true purpose, regardless of how we were born. Feminism gave me the courage to express my emotions more freely.

It gave me an obsession to share the stories only I can share with you. It has given me a freedom I never knew before. I'm no longer afraid of being seen as who I truly am. Feminism will liberate both women and men from prescribed gender stereotypes all over the world.

Author Bronnie Ware's life transformed when she spent time with people who were close to departing this life. In her book, *The Top Five Regrets of the Dying*, the most common regret was that people wished they had been true to themselves.

Once we acknowledge that limited time is remaining, although we don't know if that is years, weeks, or hours, we are less driven by ego or by what other people think of us. Instead, we are more driven by what our hearts truly want. This acknowledgment of our inevitable, approaching death, offers us the opportunity to find greater purpose and satisfaction in the time we have remaining.[87]

If you were on your deathbed today, knowing that you were going to die tomorrow, how would you measure your life? Your time is limited, so live every moment intentionally. If you don't set your own agenda, someone else will. If you don't fill your schedule with things you believe are important, other people will fill it for you.

---

87 Bronnie Ware, *The Top Five Regrets of the Dying* (Carlsbad, Hay House Inc., 2012).

Your life is not measured by how well you play a role given to you at birth. True value comes from who you are, not what you own. Life is about connection through relationships. It's about the capacity to love and be loved.

Are you ready to live the life you are meant to live?

CONCLUSION

FREEDOM
LIBERATE YOUR SOUL

"The world of humanity is possessed of two wings: the male and the female. So long as these two wings are not equivalent in strength, the bird will not fly."

—ABDU'L-BAHÁ

Imagine it's your one hundredth birthday.

Yes, you have lived that long, and you are healthy. Today, you are celebrating one century of a true and beautiful life.

How does it look? How does it feel?

What is most important to you? What do you value the most?

What are you grateful for? Who are you for the people in your life?

At your birthday dinner, you are surrounded by people you love. You may even have letters from loved ones who have already passed. Everyone is seated and raising their glass. One person stands up and shares something about you she or he is thankful for. A second stands up and toasts your passion. Finally, a third person ends the series of toasts by sharing what she or he appreciates about the contribution you have made to the world.

What do they tell you? What do the messages in the letters say about you?

Take some time to write it down on a piece of paper.

Mark Twain said, "The two most important days in life are the day you were born and the day you found out why." I found out why I was born on the day I first did this exercise at a leadership development course I attended in June 2017. I saw the ending of my life and felt how I'd like to feel when I'm preparing to leave this world. Since that day, I have known how I want to live for the rest of my life.

In the contribution section, I wrote, "Living a life I truly desire and helping others do the same with their lives."

What do I truly desire? It's freedom. What I want most in life is freedom of time, which is the most valuable currency on this planet. We all have limited time in our lives. Some of us may live to one hundred years, which is 1,200 months or 5,200 weeks or 36,500 days or 876,000 hours, and most of us have already lived a big chunk of it. When I put it this way, life seems too short to waste time on activities I don't enjoy. I want to spend every minute of my life doing more of what matters and loving who I am and what I do.

I love spending quality time with my family and close friends. I love to take care of myself through exercise, meditation, healthy eating, and sleep. I love to travel and explore the world. I love to read, to learn new skills, and discover different perspectives. I love to connect with others through sharing our stories and points of view.

I chose to write this book to spread my message. After 46,000 words and countless hours before work and on weekends over a three-year period, I turned in my manuscript—only to get my feelings hurt by my editors. Without the amazing work of those talented and candid editors, who refused to let me publish a bad book, you wouldn't be reading this book now.

How can this book help you live the life you truly desire? There were many moments I doubted I could finish it. I wasn't sure whether anyone would actually care about what I wanted to say. But I kept believing that I needed to share my story. It is my responsibility to let the world know my point of view on the subject of gender equality. As a man, it is my responsibility to share how the pursuit of gender equality has transformed my life with other men. Now it's your turn.

As the renowned author, Stephen King, says, "Writing isn't about making money, getting famous, getting dates, getting laid, or making friends. In the end, it's about enriching the lives of those who will read your work, and enriching your own life, as well."[88]

The process of writing has been a tremendous experience for me. Even before selling any copies of this book, it has already enriched my life. I hope it will enrich yours as well.

You might be wondering about the title of the book. From the story I have shared so far, it looks as though my partner and I combined our birth names. The reason why this book is called *I Took Her Name* is because that's what happened when I changed my last name in Japan. In my home country, we didn't have the option to combine our birth names to create a new last name. As I write this, Japan only allows married couples to have one last name.[89] So,

---

88 Stephen King, *On Writing: A Memoir of the Craft* (New York, Scribner, 2010).

89 "選択的夫婦別姓氏制度," Ministry of Justice, accessed September 21, 2020, http://101.110.15.201/MINJI/minji36.html.

my wife officially changed her name in the United States, her home country, and then I literally registered her whole new last name in my family registry in Japan.

Who cares? No one needs to care why I changed my name. If you're still reading this book, you might not be ready to change your name, but I know you are ready to change your life.

Changing my name changed the way I see the world. Through this journey, I experienced the culture I grew up in from a woman's point of view. I'm now more aware of gender expectations in my everyday life.

Pause for a moment and pay attention to your everyday life. What gender expectations do you see around you? How do you feel about them? When you let go of those expectations, you will start to write your own script. You may have locked yourself in a cage of expectations. But the very same cage with the door open is a home. It's your job to unlock that door. No one else will do it for you.

Ask yourself if you're living your life the way you truly want. If not, ask yourself, "Why do I feel this way and what can I do about this?" Choice happens when we take full responsibility for our lives. We live in a world full of choices, and we can create any life our hearts truly desire.

For me, officially adding those four letters at the end of my birth name symbolizes the power of choice, along with my belief that although women and men are biologically different, we can achieve equality together. We don't need to play our gender—we can be who we want to be no matter what gender we are born with. Becoming Matsuo Post is my way of taking action for my beliefs.

One important note: I am not anti-Japan. I love my home country and am incredibly proud to be Japanese. Because I love Japan so much, I want to contribute to a better, more equal future for its people. For those who believe Japan doesn't need to get better, I have no intention to offend or patronize you in any way. In many aspects, Japan is as great as a country gets when it comes to cleanliness, delicious food, customer service, and in many other ways. But when it comes to gender equality, we have a long way to go. The statistics don't lie.

Some countries might be closer to achieving gender equality than others, but sexism remains present everywhere in the world. We need to question our pre-existing gender expectations and focus on being human.

Feminism isn't solely about empowering girls and women. It is also about freeing us men to express our feelings more vulnerably. We can say no to the scripts given to us when we were born. We can choose to live whatever scripts we put our minds to. We can write our own scripts. We can set ourselves free.

The best thing a man can do to help feminism is to educate other men. I'm not trying to lecture men or tell them who to be; I share what I know because I want other men to be free to become who they truly are.

This journey has made me fully aware of the power of choice; we can do anything if we put our heart and soul into it. Society, however, doesn't allow us to make those choices easily. Feminism is about the liberation of humankind through equality. It's a belief that every human being, regardless of gender, has the choice to do what she or he wants. Every person in this world should choose to be whatever she or he wants to be. Meaningful change always begins with an indestructible belief.

Achieving equality is only the beginning. The ultimate goal of humanity is connection. We are here to belong, regardless of our race, religion, or gender. We are here to love each other.

Some men may advocate feminism by saying, "As a father of a daughter," or "I have a sister." No man needs a daughter or sister to support feminism. At this point, I don't have a sister or a daughter, but I am pro-feminism. I plan on having children in the future. Regardless of their sex, I will raise them to be feminists.

There is more to the quotation by Abdu'l-Bahá mentioned in the beginning of the chapter. It continues as follows:

> "Until womankind reaches the same degree as man, until she enjoys the same arena of activity, extraordinary attainment for humanity will not be realized; humanity cannot wing its way to heights of real attainment. When the two wings...become equivalent in strength, enjoying the same prerogatives, the flight of man will be exceedingly lofty and extraordinary."

Even if all women were feminists but men didn't actively support gender equality, all of our lives would be diminished. It is crucial that we men carry the torch of feminism and challenge patriarchy. The extinction of patriarchy will not lead to a fictional matriarchy where all-female Amazonians fight the villains to save humankind. It will lead to a powerful democracy where thinking, feeling, learning, and different types of relationships are encouraged for all people.

The battle of the sexes is never about fighting against each other. We are meant to win this battle together. As the two halves of humanity form a truly equal partnership at all levels of society, both women and men will lift each other up, respecting and appreciating our unique differences.

Believe in feminism simply because we are human and

it benefits both women and men. It's time for you to call yourself a feminist, call out sexism, and promote gender equality.

If all men around the world believed in gender equality and took meaningful action, the word feminism wouldn't even need to exist.

"I'm not a feminist. I'm an equalist," our future generation may say. Until that day comes, let's just all be feminists. For our freedom.

EPILOGUE

"Expectations will not be set by gender but by personal passion, talents, and interests."

—SHERYL SANDBERG

I started writing this book in the fall of 2017, shortly after my wife and I got married. Since we got engaged, we've been talking about having children.

As I began my second draft, my wife became pregnant with our first child. We are expecting a child in the fall of 2020, around the same time this book is scheduled to launch. About three months into her pregnancy, I decided to talk to my employer about taking extended parental leave. I had done extensive research on the topic, thought long and hard about what I wanted, and knew my actions would align with my beliefs. Nonetheless, I was incredibly nervous broaching the subject with my boss. I was asking for a lot of time. How long? Seven months. No man in my company had taken more than two weeks off for parental leave. It was unprecedented.

Before meeting my boss, I reached out to the director of Fathering Japan. Despite all I thought I knew, I needed reassurance that the law was on my side and that my job would be protected. I needed advice from someone who had been through what I was about to undergo. I took notes on what to do if my employer pressured me to come back sooner and felt reassured by the camaraderie of a fellow father.

> "If your employer is hesitant to agree to you taking seven months off at once," he said, "know that in Japan, fathers can take childcare leave twice within the first year, as long as you take time off in the first eight weeks after your child's birth. This strategy might work better, since it might show your commitment to your employer more than just taking one long leave."

Gulp. It sounded like negotiating for a salary. It made me even more nervous. Nonetheless, he gave me the encouragement I needed, telling me I was making history for the men at my company. I needed to hold my ground and confront gender expectations.

The day came. My boss sat on a stool in a meeting room

at our office and we looked at each other over a high table. My heart was pounding. I came into the room ten minutes early to go over my notes. Why was I so nervous?

"My wife is pregnant and we are expecting our child in September," I started. "I would like to take some time off for childcare leave."

"Is this your first child?" he asked.

"Yes."

"Congratulations," he said with a broad smile. "I'm really happy for you and your wife. How long do you want to take off?"

I told him I wanted to leave at the end of August and come back at the beginning of April. A total of seven months. The moment of truth.

"I want you to do whatever you and your wife decide to do," he said, looking me in the eye. "Send me an email explaining the days you want to take off. And don't worry about your position while you are away—that's for me to worry about."

My shoulders dropped. I exhaled. A huge relief. I had wasted so much energy. Later that week, I sent an email to him with the exact dates I was planning on leaving and coming back. He responded within minutes: *Approved.*

Granted, I live in a country that provides up to twelve months of paid (up to a certain percentage of salary) childcare leave to all mothers and fathers. However, as I mentioned earlier in the book, 85 percent of men in Japan wish to take paternity leave, but only 6 percent actually took it in 2018. Additionally, of the 6 percent of men who took paternity leave, 75 percent took two weeks or less.

Most men don't even ask for paternity leave, fearing rejection from their employer, poor performance reviews, and fewer career opportunities in the future. I knew all about these preconceived ideas, and yet these thoughts still came to my mind. I never knew how simple it was to secure parental leave until I asked.

We need more countries to set up systems that allow men to take as much childcare leave as women. More importantly, we need to create a culture that encourages men to actually *take* extended childcare leave. To be effective, it needs to be normalized.

More than anything, I'm beyond excited to take care of my first child full time with my wife during our parental leave. I'm also nervous. I feel like I'm starting a new job in a completely different industry:

- **Job title:** Dad
- **Responsibility:** Taking care of a human being 24/7 with your partner
- **Compensation:** -$233,610 (the estimated cost of raising a child through age 17, according to the USDA[90])

Thinking out loud, maybe I'd rather be at work. Maybe I *should* be working harder to save for the negative compensation of raising a child. I can hear a monster voice in my head: *Are you making a big mistake?*

The optimist in me says: *It's going to be the greatest experience that money can't buy.* Maybe I'll love it so much that I'll drop out of the workforce entirely and devote myself to childcare full time, joining the 7 percent of fathers who work full time inside the home.[91]

Maybe it's good that I'm highly competitive. Since most people still believe women are better at raising children than men, I'm going to challenge that status quo. I will be one of those parents with a sporty stroller running around a park and using the child as a free weight to do squats. I will be the super dad who dives in headfirst to dirty diapers

---

90 Mark Lino, "The Cost of Raising a Child," U.S. Department of Agriculture, published February 18, 2020, https://www.usda.gov/media/blog/2017/01/13/cost-raising-child.

91 Gretchen Livingston, "Stay-at-home moms and dads account for about one-in-five U.S. parents," Pew Research Center, published September 24, 2018, https://www.pewresearch.org/fact-tank/2018/09/24/stay-at-home-moms-and-dads-account-for-about-one-in-five-u-s-parents/.

and plays with rubber duckies during bath time. I'll do the night shift for my wife.

As I write this, my wife is more than halfway into her pregnancy. She and I decided not to discover the child's sex until its birth. From the moment of birth, the child will be gendered whether we like it or not. From clothing to burp cloths to furniture, pink and blue will be smeared across our child by loving friends and family and a society that offers few other options. That process does not need to start in the womb.

Our greatest hope is that our children, regardless of their gender, will be able to choose whom they want to be without internal or external obstacles forcing them to question their choices. We hope they will live in a society that respects the choices of every individual. From supporting men who choose to do the important work of raising children full time to women who choose to work full time outside their home to lead a community, a city, or even a country. The choice should be that: a choice.

And when they find where their true passion lies, we hope they will fly out to the world in freedom, like a bird with two equally capable wings.

ACKNOWLEDGMENTS

"The root of joy is gratefulness...It is not joy that makes us grateful; it is gratitude that makes us joyful."

—DAVID STEINDL-RAST

Writing a book is harder than I thought and more rewarding than I ever could have imagined. Throughout the past three years, I considered quitting countless times. But the encouragement from my family, friends, coworkers, and my publishing team kept pushing me to finish the book. For that, I'm eternally grateful.

First, my sincere gratitude and appreciation goes to you, reader. Of all the books you could read, you chose this one and I don't take that lightly. Thank you. Your support means the world to me.

To the amazing tribe at Scribe Media. Once I decided

to work with you, the process was automatic. You held me accountable throughout the editing, publishing, and marketing processes, so I couldn't *not* publish this book. Special thanks to Kayla Sokol, my publishing manager who guided me with patience throughout my entire journey with Scribe Media; Rob Petersen, my editor who coached me to sharpen my message as clear as possible; Rachael Brandenburg, my art director who created the most striking book cover I could ever ask for; and Miles Rote, my marketing strategist who helped me create a plan to get my message out to the right readers around the world.

To my mom and my dad for accepting me for who I am and sending me off to the US at age fifteen. Now that I'm about to be a parent, I can't imagine sending my child to a foreign country at that young age. You have guided me, encouraged me, loved me, and consoled me through it all. Thank you for always believing in me.

To my brother, for all the laughter, tears, high fives, and fist bumps. I don't know if I could have been as adventurous as I was if I didn't have a close older brother who showed me the ropes.

To the Post family, for taking me in as a family member. I wouldn't have added those four letters if it wasn't for this loving and kind family. Thank you for all of your love and support.

To Greg Goble, for reading my early drafts and giving me advice on how I could make the book better. Greg, you are the only person who read my very first draft front to back and gave me feedback. Thank you for all the time you spent on reading my drafts and being a great friend.

To Melanie Valesi, Menya Hinga, and Brendan Vaughan, for your candid feedback on the first few chapters of my first draft and your specific suggestion on how to make the book better. I hope you have enjoyed the final manuscript much better.

To Jason Basa Nemec, for being my role model and giving me tips on fatherhood and being a man. When I become a parent soon, I aspire to be a kind and mindful father as you are. The world's problems would be far fewer if more men were like you.

To Manabu Tsukagoshi, Soichiro Nishimura and Noriaki Wada, my mentors at Fathering Japan for giving me advice on promoting gender equality in Japan. Without fathers like you, the gender gap in this country would continue to widen. Thank you for leading by example and challenging the traditional role of husbands and fathers in Japan.

To Lean In Tokyo, HerStory Tokyo, and enjoi Diversity & Innovation Consulting for giving me the opportunity to speak at your events to share my story and get connected with like-minded people in Japan. Special thank you to Jackie F. Steele for writing the foreword to this book, promoting diversity in Japan, and connecting me with talented thought leaders to talk about this issue. I look forward to our future collaboration and partnership.

To my friends who helped me pick out the original book cover: Nick Corjon, Dane Benham, Jooho Kwon, Jon Hippensteel, Maha Kikugawa, Robin Lewis, and Matt Barker.

Finally, none of this was possible without my life partner, Tina. You are the reason why I have this story to share, and I'm eternally grateful for your patience with my journey to feminism when we first met. I've grown as a human more than I've ever thought was possible, because you helped me take off the mask I wore and get out of the cage I was in. I love you more than words can express.

ABOUT THE AUTHOR

SHU MATSUO POST is a feminism and zero-waste advocate, a plant-based endurance athlete, and a real estate investor. He lives in Tokyo, Japan, with his wife, Tina.

Contact Shu at itookhername@shumatsuopost.com.

Learn more at shumatsuopost.com.

Instagram: @shumatsuopost

Made in the USA
Monee, IL
14 May 2021

68612354R00152